115
5107

which?
essential guides

WHAT TO DO WHEN
SOMEONE DIES

"We are all born, and - sometime - we will all die. Those who are left behind will want to plan a suitable funeral and then take care of the estate. "

Paul Harris

About the author

Paul Harris is a retired manager of a group of funeral directors, who is still involved with the funeral profession. Before this, he trained as an electronic engineer, and later spent 25 years in the Free Church ministry. Here he organised seminars and lectured on many subjects related to bereavement care. He now writes for various national periodicals.

which?
essential guides

WHAT TO DO WHEN
SOMEONE DIES

PAUL HARRIS

Which? Books are commissioned and published by Which? Ltd,
2 Marylebone Road, London NW1 4DF
Email: books@which.co.uk

Distributed by Littlehampton Book Services Ltd, Faraday Close, Durrington,
Worthing, West Sussex BN13 3RB

British Library Cataloguing in Publication Data
A catalogue record for this book is available from the British Library

ISBN 13: 9 781 84490 028 2
ISBN 10: 1 84490 028 2

Although the author and publishers endeavour to make sure the information
in this book is accurate and up-to-date, it is only a general guide. Before taking
action on financial, legal, or medical matters you should consult a qualified
professional adviser, who can consider your individual circumstances. The author
and publishers can not accordingly accept liability for any loss or damage
suffered as a consequence of relying on the information contained in this guide.

Author's and publisher's acknowledgements
The author and publishers would like to thank Hilary Fenton-Harris, Health care
Manager at Poole Hospital NHS Trust, together with the team at UK Transplant
for contributing material on organ donation, Paul Elmhirst, Jonquil Lowe, Gavin
McEwan of Turcan Connell for advice on the law in Scotland, and all those who
have provided information and given invaluable assistance.

Edited by: Emma Callery and Ian Robinson
Designed by: Bob Vickers
Cover photographs by: Getty/Photolibrary
Printed and bound by Scotprint, Scotland

For a full list of Which? Books, please call 01903 828557, access our
website at www.which.co.uk, or write to Littlehampton Book Services.
For other enquiries call 0800 252 100.

Contents

Introduction

When someone dies, the deceased's family have many things to think of and to do - often at a time when they are least able to attend to such maters and are still coming to terms with the pain and shock of bereavement. This book is designed to help with the practical tasks that lie ahead, from notifying the medical authorities, to sorting out funeral arrangements, seeing to financial affairs and administering a will.

The book is structured in chronological order. It begins with those things that need to be done most urgently, then moves on to matters that are less immediate but can still cause considerable anxiety and stress (see the chart opposite).

IMMEDIATE TASKS

For many readers, dealing with a death in the family is something they have never faced before. It isn't always clear who is responsible for getting things done, or who you need to talk to about what should happen next. The first few days are often confusing and difficult to get through, as paperwork and administrative procedures are added to an already heavy emotional burden. Working through the first two chapters of this book will help. You can make sure that nothing gets overlooked, from dealing with doctors and medical staff to registering the death and obtaining the correct certificates. Doing this properly at the outset will save

unnecessary stress and pressure later on. You may find it helpful to use the book as a checklist, working through each section step-by-step, then moving on to the next.

FUNERAL CHOICES

Reading about funeral arrangements will help to clarify what sort of ceremony you would like. The options nowadays range from traditional formality to far more relaxed send-offs. Most people find the advice of a funeral director helpful here – and we discuss who you should choose, what you can expect from them, and how much everything will cost.

The book is written with people's differing needs in mind, from those whose religion calls for special observances and procedures, to those who seek non-traditional funerals, with a minimum of ceremony.

In particular, we consider the needs of Buddhists, Hindus, orthodox Jew, Muslims and Sikhs, and how they can ensure that any special requirements

An overview of the contents of this book

This breakdown of what you need to be aware of assumes the most straightforward of scenarios. When there is a coroner involved, events become slightly more complicated (see pages 23-32).

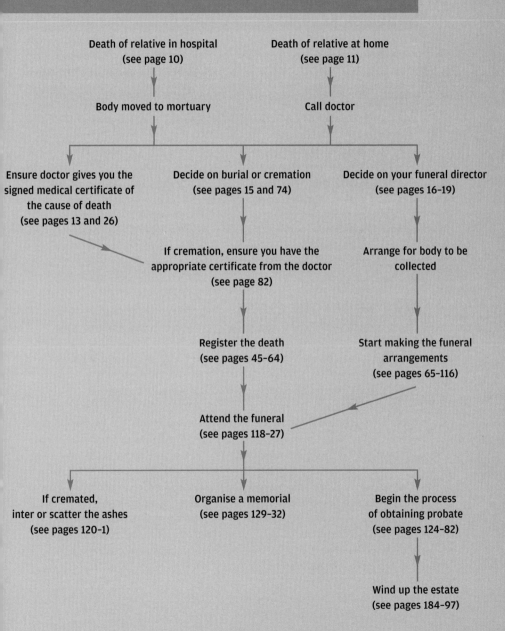

Death of relative in hospital
(see page 10)

Death of relative at home
(see page 11)

Body moved to mortuary

Call doctor

Ensure doctor gives you the
signed medical certificate of
the cause of death
(see pages 13 and 26)

Decide on burial or cremation
(see pages 15 and 74)

Decide on your funeral director
(see pages 16-19)

If cremation, ensure you have the
appropriate certificate from the doctor
(see page 82)

Arrange for body to be
collected

Register the death
(see pages 45-64)

Start making the funeral
arrangements
(see pages 65-116)

Attend the funeral
(see pages 118-27)

If cremated,
inter or scatter the ashes
(see pages 120-1)

Organise a memorial
(see pages 129-32)

Begin the process
of obtaining probate
(see pages 124-82)

Wind up the estate
(see pages 184-97)

are recognised and acted on accordingly. These may create practical difficulties but with adequate planning these can be kept to a minimum and dealt with calmly and effectively.

As well as funeral services, cremation, burial and memorials are all covered in detail. The practicalities of arranging these are considered, with alternative options clearly set out. Personal preferences, religious beliefs and cultural factors play an important part in these decisions and the book acknowledges their significance in a way that encourages readers to make their own choices rather than feeling pressured into standard solutions.

SORTING OUT THE ESTATE

After the funeral, there is a new set of problems to contend with, as the estate of the deceased is wound up and their final wishes attended to. Those responsible face a drawn-out process, which many can find demanding (particularly if they decide to go it alone rather than employing a solicitor). The additional paperwork can seem daunting, but *What to Do When Someone Dies* explains what you need to do to make things go smoothly – and indicates when the best course of action is to seek professional advice.

Executors are given clear guidance on how to go about applying for probate, what to do about financial matters and how to fulfill the terms of a will. Problem areas are discussed in a way that non-experts will find helpful, from inheritance tax to disputed claims. Readers are encouraged to check that key tasks have been completed at each stage – allowing you to stay on top of things, to assess how much progress you have made, and to work out what remains to be done. Flow charts guide you through over legal and financial hurdles, while go-further boxes at the foot of the page show sources of additional information you can access over the internet or elsewhere in the book. Regular 'Jargon buster' boxes help to demystify the technical and legal terms you will encounter at different stages. These are also summarised in a full-length glossary at the end of the book.

A final section outlines what benefits are available for those left alone after bereavement and there are addresses and website details of organisations to contact.

No one can remove the heartache of bereavement, but we hope that *What to Do When Someone Dies* will make proceedings less stressful and more straightforward. By following its advice you can confidently follow through the whole process, from start to finish, with a ready source of reference to turn to whenever you need practical guidance.

When someone dies

Coming to terms with the death of a loved one is something that needs time. Planning the funeral can be helpful in the short-term because it gives the bereaved relatives something else to focus on. Here, guidance is given on what you first need to think about, from deciding on a burial or cremation to the practicalities of paperwork.

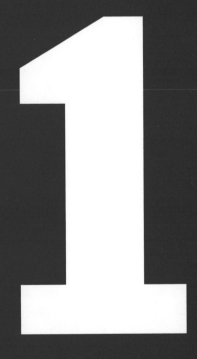

The first steps

All of us will, at some time, experience bereavement as a member of the family or a close friend dies. Depending on the circumstances, there are a few actions that need to be taken immediately.

DEATH IN HOSPITAL

The great majority of deaths now occur in hospitals or nursing homes. Most nursing staff usually have a good idea of when a patient is likely to die, and will call relatives to the hospital, if they are not already there, so that they may be present when the death occurs. If this is not possible, the relatives, or whoever was named as next of kin when the patient was admitted, will be informed of the death by the ward nursing staff, or the hospital's bereavement officer.

If a death occurs in the evening or the middle of the night, the body of the deceased person will be moved to the hospital mortuary, and an appointment made with the relatives to deal with the formalities on the following day. The deceased's possessions will have to be removed from the hospital, and these can usually be collected from the hospital's property office by the next of kin or his or her authorised representative. A letter of authorisation may be necessary, and a signature will be required.

 Sometimes, the person who died may not be an in-patient at the hospital, but may die while attending the Accident and Emergency department, or an outpatients clinic. In such cases, a member of the family will probably be asked to identify the body.

If death was unexpected, the result of an accident, or occurred during an operation or while the patient was recovering from an anaesthetic, the coroner must be informed and will investigate the cause of death (see pages 23–33). Normally, all deaths taking place within 24 hours of an operation or admission to the hospital will be reported to the coroner. Many coroners require such referrals to be made as a matter of course, with a view to ensuring that a death that may be due to unnatural causes is not missed.

DEATH AT HOME OR IN A NURSING OR RETIREMENT HOME

If the doctor has been in regular attendance, and the person concerned has been expected to die, you do not need to call the doctor immediately, unless there is any doubt at all that death really has occurred. Similarly, should a terminally ill person die at home in the middle of the night, there is no need to inform the doctor until early the following morning.

If the death has been peaceful and expected, the doctor may not feel it necessary to come, or at least not straight away. If the doctor does not intend coming, ask his or her permission for a funeral director to remove the body, which may not be done otherwise.

If a decision has already been made that the funeral will involve cremation, you should tell the doctor at this point as papers will need to be prepared, which will involve the doctor examining the body and arranging for another doctor to perform a similar examination. Some doctors make a point of seeing the body of every patient who has died as soon as is convenient. However, the doctor may prefer to examine the deceased at the funeral director's mortuary, in which case (with the doctor's permission) the

Relatives at hospital
All hospitals have considerable experience of dealing with bereaved relatives, and the staff appointed to this duty are usually patient and sympathetic. However, demands on nurses' and doctors' time are considerable, and emergencies often arise; it is thus likely that, from time to time, some waiting may be involved. The hospital will do its best to make its procedures clear, and most now publish bereavement booklets, which contain essential information for bereaved relatives.

body may be removed by the appropriate funeral director.

If the body is to be kept at home until the funeral, keep the relevant room as cool as possible. In hot weather, it may be advisable to keep the body cool by using cloth-wrapped ice packs.

UNEXPECTED DEATH

Unless the person concerned had been ill and death was partly expected, call the emergency services for an ambulance immediately.

In this situation, when the paramedics arrive and confirm death,

 In the aftermath of death it can feel quite bewildering, especially because there are a lot of decisions that need to be made relatively quickly. The services of a good funeral director can be invaluable at this time - see pages 16-19.

the police and coroner will be informed, and the body will be taken to the coroner's mortuary for examination (see pages 27–8).

It can sometimes be difficult to tell whether a person is really dead or not; for instance, someone rescued from water may appear not to breathe, yet may be revived by artificial respiration. The shock of the encounter must not prevent you from trying to find out whether the person is still alive or not. Follow these basic principles:

- **Make sure it is safe to approach:** for instance, is the person touching an electric cable? If so, don't touch him or her – call the emergency services immediately
- **Check for signs of life** by shaking and shouting at the person to try to get a response
- **Look, listen and feel** to check for breathing
- **If the person is not breathing,** look for other signs of life: check his or her colour and body temperature and try to feel for a pulse. Someone who has been dead for a few hours will be much colder than usual, but a low body temperature alone is not a sure sign of death.

If there is any doubt whether someone is dead, treat him or her as still being alive. Take great care in examining any person found apparently dead out of doors: someone may appear to be dead, but in reality be still alive and suffering from injuries that could prove fatal if he or she were moved.

Calling the police

If you think that death appears to have been caused by an accident or violence, or to have occurred in other non-natural or suspicious circumstances, you must inform the police at once. The police will inform the coroner.

Do not touch or move anything in the room, or allow anyone else to do so, until the police say that you may. The police will almost certainly want to take statements from anyone who was with the deceased when he or she died, or who discovered the body, but no one is obliged to give a statement to the police. If there is an inquest later, anyone who has made a statement may be called as a witness, as may any person whom the coroner believes may be able to give information about the death.

If a body cannot be identified immediately, the police circulate a description in police journals, and occasionally to the general press, too. Anyone who might be able to identify the body usually has to go to the mortuary with the police.

If the police are called and no relative or other person responsible is immediately available, the police take possession of any cash or valuables. As a general rule, this property is given up to whoever can later prove the right to it. The police also take away any article that may have a bearing on the cause of death – a letter or bottle of pills, for example – in case this is needed by the coroner.

ORGAN DONATION FOR TRANSPLANTATION

Organ transplantation is one of the greatest medical success stories of our time. Kidney, liver, heart and heart-lung transplants have now become routine operations, and the process is constantly being developed. In the UK in 2005, 2,796 patients had their lives saved or improved by organ transplantation.

The overall effectiveness of the transplant programme is limited by the fact that the demand for organs still far exceeds their availability. Today, nearly 7,000 people in the UK are registered for an organ transplant, most for a kidney but others for a heart, liver or lungs. However, still fewer than 3,000 transplants are carried out each year: last year almost 500 people died while awaiting a transplant.

Most organ donors are patients who die as a result of a severe head injury, brain haemorrhage or stroke and who are maintained on a ventilator. Patients who die in this way are able to donate organs and tissues for transplantation. Patients whose death is confirmed by the heart stopping beating and who die in hospital but are not maintained on a ventilator can, in some circumstances, donate organs and tissues for transplantation.

The organs that are most commonly used for transplantation are:

- **The kidney:** Each year over 2,500 patients in the UK develop chronic renal failure; kidney transplantation saves many lives.
- **The liver:** Liver transplants have been successfully carried out in the UK since 1968.
- **The heart:** The first heart transplant in the UK was carried out in 1968. Heart transplantation is considered for patients with severe cardiac failure, where further surgical and/or medical treatments are no longer possible.
- **Heart and lung:** The first heart and lung transplant in the UK took place in 1985. Heart and lungs can be transplanted together or separately, depending on the patient's condition.
- **The pancreas:** Transplantation of the pancreas may be offered for some patients with Type-1 diabetes.

Body donation

A number of people express the wish that their body should be used after death for medical research. Bodies donated in this way are used by doctors and medical students who are studying and researching the structure and function of the normal human body. If such a wish was expressed by the deceased, the next of kin or executor should immediately telephone HM Inspector of Anatomy for details of the relevant anatomy school. Tel: 020 7972 4551/4342 or go to www.doh.gov.uk and key in HMIA into the search box.

13

- **Eyes (tissues):** Corneal damage is a major cause of blindness, but thousands of people have now had their sight restored by a cornea transplant.
- **Heart valves (tissues):** The whole heart is donated for the heart valves to be suitable for transplantation.
- **Other transplants:** Other tissues that can be transplanted include skin, bone, connective tissue, major blood vessels, foetal cord blood cells and bone marrow.

The NHS UK Transplant keeps an Organ Donor Register, which is a confidential, computerised record of the wishes of people who have decided that, after their death, they want to leave a legacy of life for others. It remains very important that family and friends should be informed of an individual's wishes, so that they are in no doubt should the time ever come. Further information is available at www.uktransplant.org.uk or phone the organ donor line on 0845 60 60 400. A leaflet entitled *Organ Donation. Your Questions Answered* is available free of charge from this number.

 If you know the funeral is to involve cremation, two doctors must examine the body and complete a certificate of examination – see pages 81–3.

MEDICAL CERTIFICATE OF THE CAUSE OF DEATH

Every death that occurs in the UK must be registered at the local registrar's office within five days (see pages 46–64) and for this to happen the registrar will require a medical certificate of the cause of death. Normally, the doctor who has been attending the deceased will sign the certificate.

When a death occurs in hospital

In the great majority of deaths in hospital, the cause of death is known to be due to natural causes. In these circumstances a hospital doctor fills out the medical certificate, which states (to the best of the doctor's knowledge):

- **The cause or causes of death** and the last date on which he or she saw the patient alive
- **Whether or not a doctor** has seen the body since death occurred.

This will usually be given to the family in a sealed envelope, together with a small form that gives basic details about registering the death. No charge is made for the certificate and it is this certificate that is used to register the death.

Hospital procedures differ, but it is usually the administrative rather than the medical staff who provide the medical certificate of the cause of death, and make arrangements with the relatives for the patient's belongings to be collected.

If the person died before a hospital doctor had a chance to diagnose the cause, then the deceased patient's own doctor may be asked to issue the medical certificate. However, if the GP feels that there is reasonable doubt as to the cause of death, he or she will be unable to sign the certificate, and the matter will be referred to the coroner. When the coroner is involved, it will not be possible for a doctor to issue a medical certificate of the cause of death, unless the coroner's consultations with the hospital and/or the patient's GP show beyond any reasonable doubt that the patient died from natural causes. In such cases, a post mortem examination (see pages 19–21) will not normally be required, and the medical certificate will be completed as normal and given to the next of kin.

If the medical certificate of the cause of death can be issued at the hospital, the relatives of the deceased person will then have to arrange for his or her body to be collected from the hospital mortuary. This may be done through a funeral director (see pages 16–19) or by the relatives or friends.

If the coroner becomes involved, however, the responsibility for the body lies with the coroner's office rather than with the hospital; the hospital will tell the relatives how to contact the coroner's office. The coroner, through his or her coroner's officer, will then provide relatives with the necessary information. The government's review on the work of the Coroner Services has recommended changes to this procedure, but none of these is in force at the time this book went to print, nor are likely to be implemented in the immediate future.

When a death occurs at home

If the doctor knows the cause of death, he or she will provide the relatives with the medical certificate (see page 11).

If the doctor is uncertain for any reason about the actual cause of death or has not seen the patient within a period of 14 days before death occurred (28 days in Northern Ireland), he or she cannot sign the medical certificate. In such cases, the coroner must be informed (see page 24) – the coroner's officer will normally contact the family and explain procedures.

The body will then be taken to the coroner's mortuary (usually at a local hospital) where the cause of death will be investigated, which may or may not involve a post mortem examination

 Orthodox Jews are never cremated, and embalming or bequeathing a body for medical purposes is not allowed (see also pages 109 and 124). Likewise, Muslims are always buried and never cremated. Traditionally, there isn't a coffin either, but see also page 125. Hindus and Sikhs are always cremated.

(see pages 27–8). In such cases, the period for registration may be extended, but the registrar must be informed of the circumstances so that appropriate action can be taken. The relatives arranging the funeral should do this (see page 80).

CREMATION OR BURIAL?

You will need to decide on whether the funeral will be a cremation or burial reasonably quickly because this will affect what certificates you need to take to the registrar – see page 80.

Sometimes the deceased will leave specific requests about his or her funeral in the will. If the deceased left no specific instructions, the decision about burial or cremation is normally made by the next of kin, or the executor. Although it is usual to carry out the wishes expressed by the deceased, there is no legal obligation to do so. Should it prove impossible to trace either a living relative or a friend willing to act as executor, the hospital or the local authority will provide a minimum-price funeral.

THE FUNERAL DIRECTOR

Whether the funeral is to involve burial or cremation, many of the arrangements can be made by a reasonably capable individual who knows what to do. However, most people feel the need of professional help at this time, and it is still rare for a funeral to be carried out without the services of a funeral director.

Choosing a funeral director is usually down to personal recommendation – ask a trusted friend who has experienced death already or a senior member of staff at the hospital or nursing home for their advice. You should also ensure the funeral director you choose is a member of one of the funeral director associations – see pages 66–9.

The funeral director can organise as much or as little as you like of the

 It is important to realise that whoever takes on the responsibility of organising a funeral will ultimately be responsible for paying the bills. You might also be the executor of the deceased person's will, but you don't have to be. You can claim the costs of a funeral from the deceased's estate (see page 71), but at the same time be aware that if the estate is insolvent you will still have to pay (see page 163).

 For more information about what makes a good funeral director, see pages 66–9. In particular, their code of conduct is described there together with the different types of service that can be supplied.

16

funeral; you don't even have to employ one at all (see box on page 18). Over the forthcoming days there will be a good deal to plan and think of, which a competent funeral director will be able to guide you through, but before you embark on that journey, the body of the deceased needs to be attended to.

Collecting the body

As soon as you have decided on which funeral director you are using, inform him or her of the situation promptly, regardless of whether the deceased died at home or in a hospital. Most funeral directors operate a 24-hour emergency service, but there is no need to inform him or her of a death that occurs in the middle of the night until the next morning.

Most hospital mortuaries are open for public business from 9am. The next of kin or executor will usually have to sign a form authorising the removal of the body to the funeral director's premises. Alternatively, the funeral director will need written authority in the form of a certificate called the 'green certificate' issued by the registrar (see page 54).

Nursing and retirement homes normally want the body moved as soon as possible.

If the body of the deceased remains at home after death, the funeral director will collect the body at a time that suits you. It is rare, nowadays, for a body to remain at home for the interval between death and the funeral, although it is possible if you request it.

When the funeral director's staff remove a body from a house or hospital, they normally use a large estate car adapted for the purpose. Sometimes an ambulance is used; very rarely, a hearse. The staff will normally use a covered stretcher; sometimes, a form of coffin designed for removals called a 'shell'.

In a hospital mortuary, the bodies are kept refrigerated; most funeral directors also have cold-storage facilities, sometimes combined with deep-freeze facilities so that bodies can, if necessary, be kept for some considerable time before the funeral takes place. This may be necessary where a member of the family is abroad and cannot be contacted or where a close relative is in hospital awaiting recovery.

Laying out the body

The initial preparation of the body for burial or cremation is called laying out; if this is done by a nurse or in hospital, it will be referred to as 'last offices', while a funeral director will refer to it as 'first offices' (because it is the last service performed for the deceased by the medical profession and the first by the funeral director). This involves washing and tidying the body, closing the eyelids and ensuring that the jaw remains closed. The hair is tidied and sometimes washed, the arms and legs are straightened and, if necessary, the body's orifices are stopped with cotton wool. A man may need to be shaved as

Making your own funeral arrangements

If you have decided to carry out funeral arrangements yourself, you must go to the hospital mortuary at an appointed time to collect the deceased's body.

You need to take with you either a suitable coffin or a stretcher, enough people to carry it, and a vehicle long enough to convey it. New Health and Safety guidelines now discourage mortuary staff from assisting with placing the body in a coffin or on a stretcher, or helping to load it on the vehicle.

the hair continues to grow for some time after death.

If laying out is done by a funeral director, the body will be dressed ready for the funeral, either in a funeral gown or, if preferred by the relatives, in everyday clothes. Many hospitals now provide only a basic laying out service, leaving the majority to be done by the funeral director.

State benefits

When a spouse or close relative dies you may become eligible for certain state benefits. See page 77 for potential help with funeral expenses and also pages 199–203 for an outline of what other state benefits are available and how to claim for them.

Laying out at home

There is a small but growing tendency for the family to arrange and conduct funerals for deceased relatives. In this case, you can do the laying out yourself at home. If someone has died at home in bed, quietly and expectedly, it is perfectly in order to rearrange the body and tidy the room. Most people still prefer to hand over funeral arrangements to a funeral director, who will then attend to the laying out. This may be done at home, if preferred; a funeral director will not normally charge extra for this service within working hours, but will usually prefer to attend to the deceased at his or her mortuary.

Chapel of rest

When the body is kept in a chapel of rest, relatives and friends can go to see it before the funeral; the funeral

For information on organising your own funeral, see 'Arranging a funeral without a funeral director' on pages 114–16.

Jargon buster

First offices When a funeral director prepares a body for burial or cremation

Last offices When a nurse prepares a body in hospital for burial of cremation

Laying out The initial preparation of a body for burial or cremation

Rigor mortis is a stiffening of the muscles, which usually begins within about six hours after death and gradually extends over the whole body in about 24 hours; after this it usually begins to wear off. Rigor mortis is less pronounced in the body of an elderly person

Hypostasis When someone has been dead for half an hour or more, parts of the skin begin to discolour with purple/black patches. It is also known as post mortem (meaning 'after death' - nothing to do with post mortem examinations) staining, and is due to blood settling in parts of the body because of gravity

 Hindus strongly object to post mortem examinations, which are held to be deeply disrespectful to the dead. Likewise, muslims usually deny permission for a post mortem or organ donation (see also pages 108-10 and 123-7).

director will usually ask for an appointment to be made so that a member of staff can be available to give the family undivided attention. Sometimes extra charges are made for viewing the body at evenings or weekends. Relatives often like to leave some personal memento in the coffin, but are embarrassed to ask; funeral directors will often suggest that photographs, letters, flowers and so on may be placed in the coffin with the deceased. Where cremation is involved, it is important that these mementoes are combustible.

While some families have no wish to visit their deceased relatives in the funeral director's chapel of rest, for others this is very important, and can assist considerably with the grief process; however, a bad appearance and odours can be extremely distressing, in which case embalming (see box, overleaf) is advisable.

Some larger firms of funeral directors also have their own chapel for private prayer, in which a religious service can be held at the beginning of the funeral before the cortege leaves for the cemetery or crematorium.

POST MORTEM EXAMINATIONS

There are two types of post mortem examination:

- The **coroner's post mortem**, which is required by law where death cannot clearly be seen to be due to natural causes. This is a statutory

Embalming

Embalming is a process intended to delay temporarily the process of decomposition, and involves replacing the blood in the arterial system with a preservative, normally a solution of formalin. The process is similar to a blood transfusion, and is sometimes called 'preservative' or 'hygienic' treatment. It has no long-term preservative value.

Embalming is advisable if the body is to be returned to a private house to await the funeral, or if the funeral is to be held more than four or five days from the date of death and the body cannot be kept in cold storage. Permission for embalming should always be obtained from the next of kin or executor after a full discussion.

In some burial schemes, such as woodland burial (see page 95), all chemicals may be prohibited; this restriction may apply to the use of embalming fluid as well as to the use of horticultural chemicals at the burial site. A 'green' embalming fluid is now available, and is gradually coming into use among embalmers. It excludes harmful and toxic chemicals and is based on organic ingredients.

Before a body can be embalmed the doctor must have completed the medical certificate of the cause of death, and the death must have been registered. Where cremation is involved, Forms B and C must also have been completed (see page 81). If the coroner is involved, embalming must not take place until his or her authority has been obtained. An embalmer should be qualified by examination, and abide by the code of practice laid down by the British Institute of Embalmers: www.bioe.co.uk.

requirement, and the consent and agreement of relatives is not required (for more information, see pages 27–8).

- The **hospital (or 'consented') post mortem**, which is usually carried out at the request of the doctors who have been caring for the deceased person, or sometimes at the request of close relatives who want to find out more about the cause of death of a family member. This is a post mortem requiring the consent of the relatives, and can be carried out only when written agreement has been obtained. If relatives agree to a hospital post mortem, the doctors will normally issue the medical certificate of the cause of death before the

 Relatives will not automatically be told the results of a coroner's post mortem, and should ask for the results if they want to know.

examination takes place, so that funeral arrangements can proceed.

Hospital post mortems

Hospital post mortems can be either:

- **Full** This involves a detailed examination of all the internal organs, including the brain, heart, lungs, liver, kidneys, intestines, blood vessels and small glands. These are removed from the body, examined in detail and then returned to the body; or
- **Limited** For those who are uncomfortable about agreeing to a full post mortem, a limited post mortem may be carried out. This involves examination only of those organs directly connected with the patient's last illness; the pathologist will examine only the organs about which agreement has been reached. This may limit the usefulness of the examination, and mean that

no information will be available about possible abnormalities present in other organs, but which may have contributed to the patient's death.

Organ and tissue retention

Pathologists who carry out a post mortem may request the retention of specific organs or tissue samples in order to enable medical staff to carry out a more detailed examination. The reasons for this may include:

- Determination of the cause of death
- Specific current research projects
- Future examination as new diagnostic techniques or fresh knowledge become available
- The education and training of medical students and doctors
- Discussions between other pathologists.

In all these ways, the retention of organs and tissue blocks can benefit

Obtaining permission for a post mortem

Hospitals wanting to carry out a post mortem examination must obtain clear and detailed consent from families of the deceased, under new guidelines issued by the Chief Medical Officer in April 2003. A number of hospitals now produce booklets on post mortem examinations for relatives, which are available on request.

Under some circumstances, relatives may be asked if they have any objection to the use of the organs of the deceased person for transplant surgery. Even if the patient had completed a donor card and enrolled on the NHS Organ Donor Register (www.uktransplant.co.uk), the relatives will be consulted before any organs are removed (see page 12).

not only the relatives of the deceased but also the wider community, by improving diagnosis, treatment and the understanding of health problems.

Retention of material

Following a coroner's post mortem (see page 27), material must be retained for as long as it has any bearing on ascertaining the cause of death; this includes sorting out any legal proceedings relating to the death. In practice, items are often retained after the coroner is satisfied for the reasons given above.

Great anxiety and concern was expressed by many after it was revealed that a number of hospitals had retained certain organs and tissue samples, removed at post mortem examinations, without the knowledge or consent of the next of kin. Because of this, new guidelines for hospital post mortems were issued in 2000, which are being constantly reviewed; the latest code of practice, *Families and Post Mortems*, was published in April 2003, and is available from the Department of Health. These guidelines make it clear to relatives that accurate information will be given to them at all times, and that their permission will be sought before the retention of any organs or tissue

samples required for further research or investigation. To assist relatives, the new guidance on post mortem practice includes a video called *Respect for the Dead* (September 2004) and examples of the new consent forms produced by the Royal College of Pathologists. Guidance about clear communication applies both to post mortem examinations ordered by the coroner, and to those agreed on between families and hospitals.

Disposal of retained material

Organs, tissue blocks (small squares of chemically treated tissue) and slides that have been retained are now required to be returned for respectful disposal if relatives want this, but the large size of many hospital archives means that checking them all takes a long time. Relatives may agree that the hospital may continue to keep such material for future use in order to benefit other patients, or ask the hospital to dispose respectfully of the organs, blocks and slides. A helpful booklet entitled *Tissue Blocks and Slides* was produced by the Retained Organs Commission. The Commission ceased to operate in March 2004, but this and other publications can be obtained from the Department of Health Publications.

The Department of Health publications website is at www.dh.gov.uk. To reach the code of practice, key 'post mortems' into the 'Search this site' window. For more information on organ donation see www.which.co.uk/whattodo.

The coroner

The office of the coroner is ancient: it originated in Saxon times and received a new emphasis under the Norman regime, when the king wanted money to pursue his holy wars.

The full title was Coronœ Curia Regis (Keeper of the Royal Pleas) and the coroner was responsible for investigating accidents such as shipwrecks – mainly to see what money could be gained for the Crown thereby – and the evaluation of treasure troves. He became responsible for keeping a record of all sudden, unexpected deaths – currently, the subject of most of the coroner's work. The modern coroner is a qualified doctor or solicitor who is paid by the local authority, but remains independent of both local and central government, being responsible only to the Crown. He or she is assisted by the coroner's officer, usually a police officer; it is the coroner's officer who is generally in contact with the public.

The government's Review of Death Certification and Coroner Services was set up in July 2001 and its report was published in June 2003. The report recommends a number of changes to improve efficiency and increase public confidence in the process of death certification and the coroner service.

None of these has been implemented at the time this book went to press, but a draft bill was laid before parliament on 12 June 2006 for pre-legislative scrutiny. The bill sees the replacement of the present 110 mostly part-time coroners by 60 full-time 'senior coroners', who will be legally qualified. They will also have smaller juries: between five and seven people rather the present seven to eleven. Juries will no longer be required for investigations into deaths caused by accidents at work or industrial diseases, also in situations where there is a risk to public safety.

❝The modern coroner is a qualified doctor or solicitor who is paid by the local authority, but remains independent and is responsible only to the Crown. ❞

A new office of 'chief coroner' will be instituted, appointed by the Lord Chancellor, to whom the senior coroners will be accountable. The chief coroner will be accountable to parliament and will be responsible for developing national standards and issuing guidelines for coroners.

At the moment, all coroners' courts are held in public: the bill makes provision for private hearings under certain circumstances, including when witnesses under the age of 17 years are answering questions. The exclusion of the public would also apply to the press, other than a single reporter who would represent the media. Families and others with significant interests will have a new right of appeal to the chief coroner against a coroner's verdict, or the decision to investigate a death.

One of the major recommendations of both the Coroner's Review and the Shipman Inquiry was that all deaths should be reported to the coroner for scrutiny before registration; this has been rejected by the government as being too expensive to implement.

Organ donation

To gain consent for organ or tissue donation (see page 12) where it is unclear whether death is due to natural causes, the coroner must be consulted. This will normally be the responsibility of the hospital consultant, and not a matter for friends or family. The coroner has the power to refuse consent to the removal or organs for transplantation if he or she feels this may adversely affect any investigation in progress.

As it will take some time for parliament to discuss the proposals of this bill, and even further to implement the training and organising of senior coroners, the situation regarding death registration and funeral arrangements is not likely to alter significantly in the near future.

DEATHS TO BE REPORTED TO THE CORONER

When a death occurs that may not be due to natural causes, it must be reported to the coroner. Even if it is fairly evident that death was due to natural causes, but the deceased had not been seen by a doctor for 14 days prior to death, or had not been seen at all by a doctor before or after death, the coroner must be informed. In Northern Ireland, the relevant period is 28 days. The coroner will then consult with the deceased's GP, who will usually be able to advise whether he or she is satisfied as to the cause of death. If the GP is satisfied that death is due to natural causes, the coroner will cease to be involved, but will send the necessary documentation to the registrar; the family will then not receive a medical certificate of the cause of death, but will be able to register the death as normal. The doctor is not legally allowed to sign the medical certificate of the cause of death if he or she has not seen the patient within 14 days, even if he or she is confident that death is due to natural causes.

In any case, where the doctor is at

all uncertain as to the cause of death, the death must be reported to the coroner. Any death attributable to industrial disease, or where compensation has been claimed because of this, must be reported to the coroner; in some cases, death caused or accelerated by injury received during military service, however long ago, must also be reported.

Other circumstances in which a death must be reported to the coroner include those when death:

- Was sudden and unexplained
- Occurred in suspicious circumstances
- Was caused directly or indirectly by any kind of accident
- Might have been due to neglect, any kind of poisoning, dependence on or abuse of drugs, or abortion
- Was by suicide
- Occurred while in prison or in police custody
- Took place during a surgical operation or before recovery from the effects of anaesthesia.

Reporting the death

Anyone who is uneasy about the apparent cause of a death has the right to inform the coroner for the district. By telephoning a police station, you can find out who the relevant coroner is and how to get in touch with him or her. Or you can give information to any local police station, which will pass the information to the coroner's officer.

The information does not have to be an allegation of some crime. There may be some circumstances that you feel are contributory to the death but may not have been known to the doctor – such as an old war wound or injury – which can be established by a post mortem examination. If you believe that the deceased may have died from some industrial disease, it is obviously best to inform the coroner before the person is cremated, otherwise the matter can never be resolved.

Generally, however, it is the doctor who reports a death to the coroner,

“Anyone who is uneasy about the apparent cause of a death has the right to inform the coroner.”

or to the police. Medical certificates of the cause of death carry a list of the type of cases that the doctor should report to the coroner. If the death comes within any of these categories, the usual practice is for the doctor to inform the coroner directly, before anyone has gone to register the death.

It may be that the registrar, when he or she gets the doctor's medical certificate of the cause of death, decides that because of the cause or circumstances of the death, he or she must report the death to the coroner. In such cases, there will be a delay before the death can be

Procedure following a death

Use this chart to establish the order of events when a coroner becomes involved in the procedings.

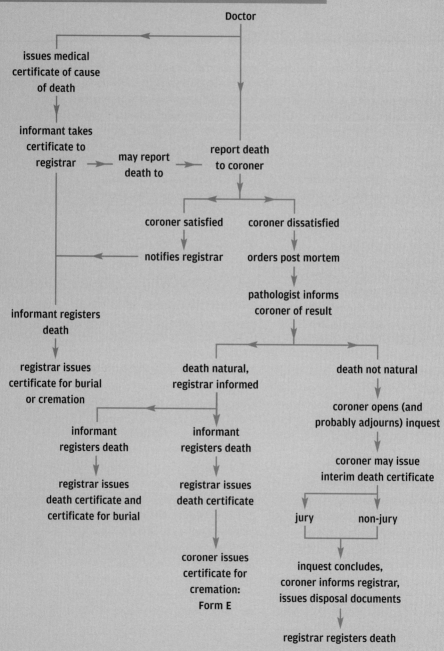

registered, which may interfere with the arrangements that the family had hoped to make for the funeral.

The coroner may decide that there is no need for further investigation, being satisfied that the cause of death is known to be natural, and that the death can be registered from the certificate provided by the doctor. In this case, the coroner sends a formal notice of the decision to the registrar of the district, and the death can then be registered in the usual way by the qualified informant. The chart opposite summarises all stages of the process. If the registrar knows who the next of kin are, he or she gets in touch with them and tells them that he or she is now in a position to register the death.

In many cases, the coroner's involvement is a formality, and reporting a death to the coroner does not inevitably mean a post mortem or an inquest. The coroner concerned will decide what action must be taken.

CORONER'S INVESTIGATIONS

When a death is reported to the coroner and he or she decides to investigate, that death cannot be registered until the coroner provides a certificate when inquiries are complete. He or she will usually order a post mortem, which will often show that death was due to natural causes; in this case, he or she will notify the family and the registrar through the coroner's officer, and the death can then be registered in the normal way.

- **If the funeral is to involve burial,** the registrar will issue a certificate for burial.

- **If it is to involve cremation,** it is the coroner who will issue a coroner's **Form E** for cremation; one part (pink) will be given to the family or sent direct to the registrar, while the other part (yellow) will be sent to the funeral director, or direct to the crematorium.

The actual funeral will have to wait for the outcome of the coroner's investigations, but in many cases the coroner's officer will be able to give a reasonably accurate indication of how long these will take. The funeral director involved will normally consult with the coroner's officer, and will be able to make tentative funeral arrangements while the investigation is proceeding: it is not necessary to wait until the investigation ends before beginning to make arrangements.

For a breakdown of all the forms that are required for registration, see pages 81–4. A description of Form E for cremations is also given on page 82.

Coroner's post mortem

More than 225,000 deaths were reported to the coroners in England and Wales in 2005, and 115,800 post mortem examinations were carried out, almost all to establish the cause of death. This may be to show that the death was due to natural causes, or it may be to resolve a dispute where the family believes that the death was caused by an industrial disease (a person may have suffered from an industrial illness for a considerable time but eventually die from some other, unrelated, cause). In a few cases, the post mortem provides valuable evidence of the manner of a criminal death.

The family of the deceased do not have to be asked to give their consent, as they would be when a hospital wants to perform a post mortem examination. The coroner arranges and pays for the post mortem.

If the post mortem reveals that the death was due to natural causes and no other circumstance warrants further investigation, the coroner notifies the registrar and the death can be registered in the usual way (see pages 45–64). In some districts, the coroner's officer or another police officer calls on the family to tell them; otherwise, the next of kin should enquire at the coroner's office every few days to find out when the coroner's notification is being sent to the registrar. The coroner has no duty to inform the next of kin of the result of the post mortem.

After the post mortem, the body

Post mortem objections

If members of the family object to a post mortem examination for religious or other reasons, or if they have any reason to believe that the examination is not necessary, they should inform the coroner. If the coroner is still of the opinion that the examination is required, the family can apply to the High Court to reverse the decision of the coroner. This will delay arrangements for the disposal of the body.

> **❝ The coroner can look at the cause of death and issue the order for burial or cremation before the inquest is held. ❞**

A hospital post mortem is usually carried out at the request of the doctors or relatives who have been caring for the deceased person. It is a way of establishing the cause of death and is described on pages 20-1.

again becomes the responsibility of the family. To avoid unnecessary delays, the family can arrange for a funeral director to collect the necessary forms from the coroner's office as soon as these are available and make arrangements for the funeral at the earliest suitable date.

IF AN INQUEST IS REQUIRED

The coroner is obliged to hold an inquest into every violent and unnatural death that is reported, and also following the death of a person in prison.

An inquest is an enquiry to determine who the deceased person was, and how, when and where that person died, and to establish the particulars that are required for the registration of the death.

An inquest is held formally and is open to the public. A person wishing to attend, but who has not been given notice of the inquest, can ask at a local police station or telephone the coroner's office to find out when the inquest is being held. The coroner may have asked for further investigations and tests to be carried out, and the date for the inquest will not be arranged until all these are complete.

Adjournment of an inquest

Coroners are increasingly prepared to open an inquest and then adjourn it 'to a date to be fixed' or for a specific

66 If an inquest is adjourned, the coroner will inform the registrar so that registration can take place and the funeral of the deceased can be arranged without too great a delay. 99

number of days. While police time is not always instantly available, this enables routine enquiries to be completed without holding up burial or cremation arrangements. If it is clear to the coroner that disposal of the body will not prejudice such enquiries, he or she can take evidence of identification and of the cause of death and may then adjourn the inquest, often for a short period, until enquiries are complete – issuing the necessary order for burial or the cremation certificate before the inquest.

Adjournments also have to be made to allow extra time in more complex matters – to await the result, for example, of an inquiry into an air crash or other disaster. The coroner may provide any properly introduced person with an interim certificate of the fact of death. This will allow insurance or other payments to be claimed and the estate to be administered.

An inquest must be adjourned where a person has been charged with causing the death or with an offence connected with it that will be the subject of a trial before a crown court jury. The coroner will then send notification to the registrar for the registration of the death.

At the court

The coroner's court is a court of law with power to summon witnesses and jurors, and with power to deal with any contempt in the face of the court.

〈〈 Tell the coroner's officer if you want to give evidence. 〉〉

Interested parties

Unlike a trial, there are no 'sides' at an inquest. Anyone who is regarded as having a 'proper interest' may ask witnesses questions at an inquest and may be legally represented. The list of people with a proper interest includes parents, children and the spouse of the deceased, insurers and beneficiaries of an insurance policy on the life of the deceased, any person whose conduct is called into question regarding the cause of death and, in appropriate cases, a chief officer of the police, a government inspector or a trade union official.

The law requires that any person with evidence to give concerning the death should attend an inquest. In practice, the coroner will have read any written statements that have been made, and will know the names of those who have been interviewed by the police and by the coroner's officers. The witnesses the coroner knows will be needed are summoned to the inquest. The summons is often an informal telephone call but there may be a written summons or a subpoena (if the witness is outside the jurisdiction of the coroner). A witness is entitled to travel expenses and to a fixed sum to compensate for loss of earnings.

If any witnesses know they cannot attend, they should inform the coroner's office at once. When a witness has been formally summoned, there are penalties for failing to attend. Non-attendance causes inconvenience, and expense, to the family if the inquest has to be adjourned.

There is a minimum amount of pomp and ceremony at an inquest. The coroner calls witnesses in turn from the main part of the court to come up to the witness box. Each witness swears or affirms to 'speak the truth, the whole truth and nothing but the truth'.

First, the coroner questions the witness; then, with his or her permission, the witness can be examined by anyone present who has a proper interest in the case (see box, opposite) (or by that person's legal representative). If you know that you will want to give evidence or examine a witness, tell the coroner's officer beforehand, so that the coroner can call you at the right moment. When all the witnesses have been heard, the coroner sums up (there are no speeches by the lawyers) and gives the verdict.

With a jury

Some inquests have to be heard before a jury. The jury is summoned in the same way as a crown court jury. In cases of industrial accidents or other incidents that must be reported to a government department, after a death in prison or in police custody or caused by the act of a police officer, and where death was in circumstances that present a danger to the public, there is always a jury.

The jury for an inquest consists of not fewer than seven and not more than 11 men or women eligible for jury service. There is no power to challenge jurors, as there is no accused person to exercise the power. The jurors are on oath. Jurors need not view the body unless the coroner directs them to.

At the conclusion of his or her enquiries, the coroner sums up the evidence to the jury and explains the law. All the findings of the inquest are then made by the jury. Jurors do not usually leave the court to discuss their decision, but they may do so. They can return a majority verdict.

The verdict

The purpose of an inquest is not only to find out who the deceased person was and how, when and where he or she came by his or her death, but also to decide the category of death. This is colloquially called the verdict, but the correct description is the conclusion. It can range from natural causes to suicide, industrial disease or misadventure. Conclusions are subject to many legal technicalities. In particular, the finding of suicide must be strictly proved: when there is no conclusive evidence of the intent to commit suicide, the coroner has to return an open verdict.

The conclusion must not appear to determine any matter of criminal liability against a named person, or any matter of civil liability.

A verdict of accidental death does not mean there will be no prosecution in a magistrates' court or that the family cannot bring an action for damages. All it means is that it is not a case of suicide or homicide. The 'properly interested persons' are entitled to a copy of the notes of the evidence and these are often useful in subsequent proceedings.

Legal advice and expenses

There should be no expense to the family arising out of an inquest. Representation by a lawyer is not necessary in the majority of inquests, and in cases where there

31

The press and inquests

Since inquests are held in public, the press can be present. There are restrictions on the publication of the names of minors, but in other matters there are no reporting restrictions.

Death is sometimes treated as a sensational subject. Although the coroner may try to choose words carefully, people giving evidence or questioning witnesses may provide comments that can be distressing to the family. The coroner will try to ensure that the facts are as accurate as possible; the inquest may be able to dispel rumours and inaccurate assertions.

is no controversy, the family should not need to incur such expense. There is no provision for representation at an inquest under the legal aid scheme.

Many people think it wise, however, to be represented by a solicitor at the inquest in the case of death resulting from an accident or an occupational disease. There may be compensation claims to be made later and a solicitor would be better able to make use of the evidence presented at an inquest.

Through your local Law Society (see below) you should be able to find a solicitor who will agree to a free or small-fee interview so that a family does not pay out money

unnecessarily. The solicitor may also be able to advise on the possibility of compensation.

After the inquest

In all cases other than those where someone has been charged with a serious offence, the coroner would already have sent an interim certificate for burial or cremation after adjournment of the inquest. However, registration of the death can usually only take place when the coroner sends a certificate after the inquest to the registrar of births and deaths of the district in which the death took place or in which the body was found (see page 46).

 INQUEST provides information and support to people facing the inquest system after a controversial death: go to www.inquest.org.uk. The organisation produces a useful pack entitled *Inquests - An Information Pack for Families, Friends and Advisors*

 Websites for finding a local solicitor are: in England and Wales: www.lawsocity.org.uk; in Northern Ireland: www.lawsoc-ni-org; in Scotland: www.lawscot.org.uk.

Special case deaths

Of course, not all deaths occur at home or in a local hospital. Sometimes people die abroad when working or on holiday. There are also the tragic incidences of a miscarriage or stillbirth. This section explains the first steps that need to be taken in these instances.

DEATH ABROAD

When someone dies abroad and the body is to be returned to the UK, the process is complex and expensive. Holiday or travel insurance that covers repatriation is essential, as the cost can run to several thousand pounds.

❝ Many consider it wise to be represented by a solicitor at the inquest into a death resulting from an accident or occupational disease. ❞

- **Those who are travelling on package holidays** should immediately contact their holiday representative: the biggest tour operators have proper procedures for handling bereavement. Further, tour operators belonging to ABTA subscribe to a code of conduct which commits them to assistance in many areas of bereavement, even where death occurs from an activity outside the normal holiday arrangements. They are also able to provide help with legal costs where necessary.
- **Those travelling independently** should ensure that their insurance covers repatriation, and be aware of the emergency telephone number on which to contact the insurance company or travel agency.

 Note that normal holiday insurance does not usually cover dangerous sports such as paragliding or scuba diving; additional cover must be taken out to cover such activities.

 For information about registering a death abroad, see page 58; and if you are arranging a funeral away from home, either in the UK or abroad, turn to pages 98–9.

" The death must be registered in the country and area concerned and the doctor's medical certificate of the cause of death and the death certificated obtained. "

The British consul in the area will be able to advise, but will not be able to help financially. The consul may be some distance from where death occurred: in the Caribbean or Greek islands, he or she may well not be on the same island. Independent travellers should also contact the local police or ambulance service as soon

Local cremation

If the deceased had no insurance and the high cost of repatriation cannot be met, local cremation may be the only option available; it will almost certainly be the cheapest option. Provided a certificate of contents is obtained from the crematorium, the ashes can be brought back to the UK as hand luggage. This option, however, is not always available: most Muslim countries have no facilities for cremation, while in Nepal bodies are normally cremated on open-air funeral pyres, which may be found unacceptable.

as possible. If there appears to be no one to advise, it would be wise to telephone a reputable funeral director in the UK to ask for advice and assistance; most funeral directors are experienced in these matters, and can turn to specialist repatriation services if they need help.

The death must be registered in the country and area concerned (see page 58), and the doctor's medical certificate of the cause of death and the death certificate obtained. The local judicial authorities may want to investigate and, in any case, authority must be obtained from them to move the body out of their country. The body must be embalmed (see page 20) before it can be moved, and a certificate of embalming will be required. The body must be contained in a metal-lined coffin, which in turn must be suitably packaged and covered with hessian. All necessary papers for customs clearance must be obtained and accompany the coffin, and arrangements should be made with an airline to convey the body to the UK – the usual method of repatriation.

Insurance companies will have contracts with repatriation services or firms of international funeral directors who will attend to all of this; if there is no insurance, it is possible for relatives to attend to the matter, but specialist knowledge and a great deal of patience are required and the matter would be better entrusted to a UK funeral director. On arrival in the

UK, customs clearance must be obtained; this may take several hours, but, once cleared, the body must be removed from the airport as soon as possible.

If death has occurred due to natural causes, the coroner will have only minimal involvement. If death is not due to natural causes, but is the result of an accident or criminal activity, the coroner in whose jurisdiction the funeral takes place will want to hold an inquest (see page 29), and the body may not be moved from the mortuary until permission is given. See also box, below.

The registrar of the district in which the funeral is to take place must be informed (see also page 58), so that a 'certificate of no liability to register' can be issued. For this, evidence of death and the cause of death will be required.

❝ You must obtain permission to move the body out of the country. The body must be embalmed and transported in a metal-lined coffin, to be covered with hessian. ❞

When the coroner is involved

If the coroner in the district orders a post mortem and he or she is satisfied that death did occur from natural causes, the necessary documents will be issued from the coroner's office.

If the funeral involves burial, the coroner will authorise a 'certificate of no liability to register', which is all that will be required.

However, if the funeral involves cremation, he or she will issue the coroner's certificate for cremation, and the Home Office will not now become involved at all.

If the coroner finds that death was, in fact, not due to natural causes, he or she will order an inquest to be held, the results of which may well be inconclusive due to the embalming or deterioration of the body and the inability to call witnesses. In such a case, the funeral cannot be held until authority to do so is received from the coroner.

DEATH AT SEA

When a death occurs on a foreign ship, it counts as a death abroad; the death must be recorded in the ship's log, and the port superintendent where the ship's crew are discharged must make enquiries into the cause of death.

When death occurs on a British-registered ship, the death is recorded in the captain's log, and all facts and particulars relating to the death must be recorded and delivered to the Registry of Shipping and Seamen (see below) on arrival at any port within or outside the UK. The master of any ship has the authority to decide whether, for health reasons, a body should be immediately disposed of at sea, or kept for disposal later. As in most of these cases the death is unexpected, the body is usually kept in order to assist with a coroner's enquiry. Most cruise ships have mortuary facilities for cold storage of those who have died on board.

When a body is brought into a British port, the death must be reported to the coroner in whose jurisdiction the port is located. He or she may decide to order an enquiry, in which case the body cannot be moved without his or her consent. The registrar of the district in which the funeral is to take place must also issue a 'certificate of no liability to register', for which either a copy of the entry in the captain's log or a death certificate must be obtained. Copies of log entries can be obtained from the shipping company that owns the ship concerned, or the port superintendent where the body was brought ashore. Copies of the death certificate may be obtained from the Registry of Shipping and Seamen. This will normally all be dealt with by the funeral director.

STILLBIRTHS AND MISCARRIAGES

Loss of the foetus before the 24th week does not fall within the legal definition of a stillbirth and is usually considered a miscarriage. If the mother was in hospital at the time, the hospital may offer to arrange for the disposal of the remains. But if the parent(s) would like these to be buried or cremated in the usual way, it should be possible to arrange this with

> **❝Many parents consider a pregnancy which doesn't come to full term deserves a dignified funeral. Some hospitals can help to organise a simple service. ❞**

 To get in touch with the Registry of Shipping and Seamen, go to www.mcga.gov.uk/c4mca/mcga-seafarer_information/mcga-rss-home.htm. For information about burial at sea, see pages 97-8.

a local cemetery or crematorium, provided a form of medical certificate is completed.

After 24 weeks, it is regarded as a stillbirth and must be registered as such. Many parents now consider a pregnancy that does not come to full term at whatever stage of gestation as resulting in a child to be mourned, and deserving of a dignified funeral. Most such sad experiences occur in hospital, and many hospitals, led by their chaplains and bereavement teams, regard all such issue as a baby, whatever the number of weeks between conception and delivery.

Some hospitals will offer grieving parents a simple cremation funeral service, possibly carried out by a funeral director contracted to the hospital, for which there may be no charge. Of course, the parents may choose to make arrangements themselves with a funeral director of their choice, in which case they will be responsible for any charges that may be incurred. Some parents may not wish to be involved in such a funeral service, in which case the hospital will arrange for respectful disposal, and later offer a service of blessing to the family concerned. Bereaved parents considering a cremation funeral for their babies and infants should be advised that

there will very seldom be any cremated remains available for later interment.

The Royal College of Nursing makes a strong case for all products of conception to be treated in such a respectful and dignified way, and parents who find themselves in such a bereft situation should discuss the matter immediately with the hospital chaplain, however difficult or painful this may be.

Retention of organs

Information in the media about the retention and disposal of organs and tissue following the post mortem examinations of babies and children has also focused attention on the disposal of stillbirths 20 to 30 years ago. Some parents have been able to trace the location of their child's burial, and appropriate memorial services on the burial site have afforded some comfort. Hospital chaplains and local funeral directors will do their best to assist parents who have anxieties in such matters.

 The Foundation for the Study of Infant Deaths (FSID) (website: www.sids.org.uk/fsid/) publishes a booklet *When a Baby Dies*, which contains lots of helpful advice. Information on registering a stillbirth is given on pagess 56-7.

The grief process

Death alters the course of daily life for all those closest to the person who has died. If someone close to you has died, you must accept that things will change, whether the change is small or immense. Something irreversible has happened and your life must now follow a different course. You will face various experiences which will affect you in certain ways until, having worked through them, you arrive at a point where your life is once again moving steadily in a positive direction.

NORMAL GRIEF

Bereavement is a very complex issue; this short section describes many of the phases that you may encounter when recently bereaved. Any description of reactions to grief has to be simplified because of the enormous variation from person to person in coping with the situation. Nevertheless, the considerable amount of study which has taken place over the last 25 years has revealed much that is common to the great majority of people.

❝Some people get stuck in the process of recovery and need help. Even family and friends often avoid those in mourning because they do not know what to say. ❞

There is nothing unusual about grieving: it is 'normal' and most people will make a 'normal' recovery without a great deal of assistance. Some, however, get stuck somewhere in the process of recovery and need help; others (fortunately, only a few) are so affected by their bereavement that the grief process gets out of hand. In such cases, treatment as well as assistance is needed, counsel as well as care. The normal grief processes only are covered in this section to help you understand how you may be feeling.

Most of the time, bereavement causes a great deal of pain; many people do not acknowledge this, fearing that they will be marked out as weak and abnormal. Family and friends will often avoid people who have lost partners, children or close friends, usually because they are embarrassed and do not know what to say. They excuse their feelings of embarrassment and helplessness by saying things like: 'Grief is a very private affair. I don't want to intrude.' So the bereaved are often deserted just when they need most support, which leads them to believe that it is their pain and tears that cause others to shun them; they therefore make determined efforts to 'be strong' and suppress their natural emotional responses. More than anything else, this hinders recovery from grief.

DEATH OF BABIES AND CHILDREN

Every year, many babies are stillborn, or die within the first month of life; approximately one couple in 500 has suffered this form of bereavement. Cot death is the sudden and unexpected death of a baby for no obvious reason, although a post mortem examination may explain some occurrences of cot deaths. Yet only in recent years have either of these experiences been recognised as real bereavement; previously parents who had lost newborn or young babies were expected to recover quickly from their losses.

Research indicates that mourning often lasts longer among bereaved parents than in widows and widowers; a survey of parents who had lost babies in the first few months of life indicated that two-thirds of those interviewed felt that their main need was to have their baby recognised as a real person, not just as 'something that could be replaced'.

❝It is only in recent years that the experience of coping with the death of a baby has been recognised as real bereavement. ❞

Memorials

Mourning involves memories and when a small baby dies, memories are few. Until very recently, it used to be felt that the less the parents knew about the dead baby, the less they would grieve; the mother was often sedated and the dead child whisked away before she or the father could see it. Relatives were advised to dispose of any potential reminders: baby clothes were removed, pram and cot disposed of and toys given away or carefully hidden. This deprived the parents of almost all the grounds of

 If you feel that you would like a memorial for your baby or child at the crematorium, cemetery or churchyard, see pages 129-32, where the many options that are available are described.

memory, thus making it almost impossible for them to find a degree of healing through mourning.

Active contact with the dead baby greatly helps to make him or her a real person to bereaved parents, and supplies at least some of the memories they need. Mothers are more often encouraged to hold their dead baby, and to wash and dress it. Photographs can provide memories and confirm the reality of a child's existence, thus providing a source of comfort. Expensive equipment is unnecessary: a simple photograph

> **" A simple photograph, lock of hair, a handprint or a footprint can provide memories and confirm the reality of the child's existence, providing some comfort. "**

Care agencies

A number of care agencies exist for the sole purpose of offering help and support to those who have lost babies and small children, and those who are trying to help parents come to terms with their loss. Compassionate Friends and The Foundation for the Study of Infant Deaths are but two of them. For contact details, see opposite.

will do. A lock of hair can be kept, or a little down snipped from the baby's head and kept in a transparent envelope. Handprints or footprints can be taken with washable ink pads, and suitably mounted. A toy or two intended for the baby can be placed with him or her in the coffin.

REACTIONS TO GRIEF

When loss has occurred and the bereaved person has been diverted from the accustomed course of life, a number of psychological forces come into effect. The different stages of grief that a person may go through include shock, sorrow, anger, apathy and depression, before the process of recovery can begin. Not everyone experiences all of these emotions, and some stages may last longer than others. In other words, everyone is different.

Shock: the primary experience

The initial effect of bereavement is shock. There is a numbness in which the rest of the world often seems to recede, leaving the bereaved person in mental limbo; a common feeling is of the world carrying on but the person no longer feeling part of it. This leads almost immediately into a stage of denial – the strong feeling that death cannot possibly have occurred, that the bereaved is dreaming, that the doctors have made a mistake. This begins at the moment of loss and has

Relief and guilt

When death occurs after a long illness, or where there was ill-feeling between the deceased and the bereaved, the initial response is a feeling of relief: the tension is at last over and done with. This may be accompanied almost at once by a sense of guilt for feeling relieved – talking about this to a sensible and trustworthy friend will help.

its major impact during the first two to three days. At this stage, people can be very susceptible; this should be recognised and great care taken when an important decision has to be made – especially the arrangements for the funeral. Dates and times often have to be decided upon quickly, but sufficient time should be allowed before the funeral to avoid making the wrong decisions in haste.

Sorrow: the underlying experience

Shock often overlaps with or is followed by feelings of sorrow – the sadness which develops as the person becomes aware that an irreversible loss has occurred. Sorrow and pining can have the effects of physical pain, often made worse by the belief that one is supposed to 'be strong' and not show any undue signs of emotional disturbance. At this point, the bereaved person needs to be free to express grief with the support of others who will not be embarrassed or try to suppress the person's tears. In order to make a good recovery, the bereaved person needs to feel this pain, express it and work through it in ways which are appropriate to his or her personality.

But initial sorrow is often accompanied by unreasonable guilt. People often feel guilty because they think they could have done more than they did – had they done more, perhaps the deceased person would not have died – and much reassurance and patience are called for. This often leads to people 'bargaining' with God or with life in general (for example, by promising to be good if only they can wake up to find that it was all a bad dream). The only way to help

To contact Compassionate Friends (see box opposite), to to www.tcf.org.uk and for the Foundation for the Study of Infant Deaths, go to www.sids.org.uk/fsid/. Both organisations have trained counsellors to give you support.

someone going through these emotions is to root the person firmly in reality, to talk about the death and to have the person visit the body in a chapel of rest, thus allowing a gradual acceptance of the situation to come about in a way that can be coped with.

The acute stage of this phase does not usually last for very long and is sometimes over in two or three weeks. The sorrow will persist but will generally subside into a numbing ache. The guilt (real or imagined) may well last for a long time.

❝Many bereaved people get angry, and have feelings of sorrow and guilt. Such emotions are often compounded by irrational resentment, even aggression. ❞

Anger: the developing experience

Many people get very angry when bereaved, usually in an irrational manner. There is anger with God (for letting death happen), with friends and family (for not understanding or for not being bereaved themselves), with themselves (for not coping) and with the deceased (for having died and left them). Sometimes the anger comes before the sorrow and guilt, sometimes after, and is often compounded by a strong and irrational resentment and a certain amount of aggression (depending on the person's personality – a very mild person is unlikely to become extremely aggressive). Friends need a great deal of patience: they should let the person cool down, then listen to the anger without being defensive or argumentative.

This stage of the grief process can last from a few days to several months. It may continue to simmer in the background for a long time, resulting in outbursts of irrational anger at unexpected times. Those on the receiving end should remember that the anger is not directed at them and should try not to feel injured or aggrieved.

 Other websites you can turn to for support are: www.childbereavement.org.uk (The Child Bereavement Trust), www.counselling-directory.org.uk (finds a local trained bereavement counsellor) and www.crusebereavementcare.org.uk.

Apathy and depression

When the anger calms down, a state of apathy often develops. The bereaved person displays indifference to what is going on round about him or her and may show a considerable reluctance to make decisions. Patience and encouragement are needed continuously.

Or there may be feelings of depression. Most people can work through these normal feelings of depression with the support of friends and family; however, this support should not be allowed to turn into an unhealthy dependence on the help of others – it is important to encourage people by doing things *with* them rather than *for* them, so that they will once again be able to do things for themselves. Occasionally, depression can degenerate into acute depression, where professional assistance is called for.

> ❝ The bereaved often become very apathetic and are reluctant to take decisions. There can also be feelings of depression. ❞

Other common reactions

- Shock can have physical effects, leading to quite genuine symptoms. These are often not recognised as being part of the normal grief process and, as a result, many recently bereaved people worry that they have a physical illness on top of the burden of bereavement.
- Headaches are common, as are a continuously dry mouth, weakness, breathlessness, oversensitivity to noise, tightness in the chest and throat, a hollow feeling in the stomach, giddiness and nausea. Hair loss may also occur. Some people lose weight, others put it on; some people are constantly tired, even when they have had sufficient sleep and food.

- There are often real feelings of fear, sometimes based on the person's anxiety that he or she will not be able to cope. Absentmindedness and lack of ability to concentrate on anything for very long are also common: sometimes people forget what they were saying in mid-sentence. Memory is frequently affected: facts, names, experiences, all well known, cannot be brought to mind when needed, which can be very upsetting.

All of these are quite normal experiences and recognising them as such will greatly assist you to live through them and come to terms with the reality of the bereavement that has occurred.

RECOVERY

Gradually, even when the pain of bereavement has been acute, a sense of acceptance grows and the bereaved person once again begins to take an interest in life. When it becomes possible for the person to make positive plans for the future and again find pleasure in everyday experience, the bereaved person is well on the way to recovery. Life will never be the same again, but it can now be lived in a normal, healthy manner.

In practice, of course, it is seldom as simple as this. Some people do not appear to go through any of the emotional phases listed above, while others pass from feeling to feeling, only to repeat the process a few weeks later. Realising that there is no one certain way that you're *supposed* to feel will help you on your way to recovery.

❝ A sense of acceptance grows, and while life will never be the same again, it can once again be lived in a normal, healthy manner. ❞

44

Registering a death

After the doctor has given you the certificate of death and you have begun planning for the funeral, you need to register the death of the deceased. This chapter looks at who, when, where and how you do this. It is a legal necessity and until the death is registered you can't proceed with the funeral plans.

Registering the death

In England and Wales, a death should be registered within five days of its happening. Registration can be delayed for a further nine days provided the registrar receives, in writing, confirmation that a medical certificate of the cause of death has been signed by the doctor.

WHERE TO REGISTER

Under English law, all deaths must be registered in the registration sub-district in which they took place or in which the body was found (the 'receiving registrar'). However, if it is more convenient, the information required may be taken to any register office in England and Wales (*not* Scotland or Northern Ireland) – the 'attesting registrar' – from which it will be passed on to the relevant register office.

Usually, whoever is giving the information goes in person to the registrar's office. An increasing number of registration districts now operate on an appointments system, although it is usually possible for you just to go along during the registrar's office hours and wait until he or she is free to see you.

Finding your local registrar

A list of names, addresses and telephone numbers of local registrars of births and deaths is usually displayed in doctors' surgeries and in public libraries and other public buildings, together with their office hours and a description of the sub-district they cover.

“By law, only relatives or certain other people can register a death, a role known as 'the informant'. ”

Registration in Scotland is slightly different to England and Wales – see pages 60–4 for information. These pages also describe the differences in the coroners' and post mortem system between Scotland and England and Wales.

WHO CAN REGISTER A DEATH?

There are only certain people who are qualified by law to inform the registrar of the details of the death which has occurred.

If the death has occurred inside a house or public building, any of the following people (described here in order of precedence) may register the death:

- A relative of the deceased who was present at the death
- A relative of the deceased who was present during the last illness
- A relative of the deceased who was not present at the death or during the last illness but who lives in the district or sub-district where the death occurred
- A person who is not a relative but who was present at the time of death
- The occupier (e.g. the matron of a nursing home or warden of pensioners' flats) of the building where the death occurred, if he or she was aware of the details of the death
- The person arranging for the disposal of the body (this means the person accepting responsibility for the funeral – *not* the funeral director, who is not normally allowed to register the death).

If the person has been found dead elsewhere, the following are qualified to register the death:

❝ The person who registers the death is known as the informant and the responsibility cannot be delegated to someone who is not qualified for that role. ❞

- Any relative of the deceased able to provide the registrar with the required details
- Any person present at the time of death
- The person who found the body
- The person in charge of the body (which will be the police if the body cannot be identified)
- The person accepting responsibility for arranging the funeral.

The person who registers the death is known as '**the informant**'. The responsibility cannot be delegated to a person who is not qualified to act as informant: should such a person attend the register office, the registrar will refuse to register the death and will require a qualified informant to attend.

In cases where a coroner's inquest has been held (see pages 29–32), the coroner will act as the informant and provide the registrar with all the necessary details. In this case, there is no need for the family and relatives to register the death, but they will need to attend the register office if copies of the death certificate are needed, or arrange for them to be sent by post.

WHAT INFORMATION IS REQUIRED

The registrar will require the following information:

- The medical certificate
- The date and place of death
- The full name and surname of the deceased (and the maiden name if the deceased was a married woman) (a marriage certificate, if relevant, would be useful)
- The date and place of birth of the deceased (the birth certificate would also be useful)
- The occupation of the deceased (and husband's name and occupation if the deceased was a married woman or widow)
- The usual address of the deceased
- Whether the deceased was in receipt of a pension or allowance from public funds
- If the deceased was married, the date of birth of the surviving partner.

((Do not fix the date for the funeral less than one week after giving information to the attesting registrar, to allow time to register the death.))

The medical certificate of the cause of death states that the deceased's National Health Service medical card should be taken and given to the registrar. However, if this cannot be found, don't delay registration: provision of the card is no longer a strict necessity.

 The medical certificate of the cause of death is the most essential item to obtain before going to the registrar – if you don't yet have it, see pages 13-15.

The medical certificate

The medical certificate of the cause of death must be submitted to the receiving registrar: if this is taken to the attesting registrar, it will be sent with other information by first-class post to the receiving registrar, who must receive it before the death can be registered. Time for this must be allowed: it is wise not to fix a date for the funeral until at least one week after giving information to the attesting registrar.

If the doctor or hospital have sent the medical certificate of the cause of death direct to the registrar, or via a funeral director, this and the information from the attesting registrar must be received by the receiving registrar before the death can be registered. Again, it is important to allow sufficient time for processing and possible postal delays if the funeral is to take place as planned.

If the registrar finds that the information the doctor has given on the medical certificate of the cause of death is inadequate or that the death was due to some cause that should have been reported to the coroner, he or she must inform the coroner accordingly and await written clearance before proceeding with the registration. He or she must also inform the coroner if it is found that the doctor had not seen the deceased within 14 days prior to death or after death.

> **❝ If the registrar finds that the information the doctor has given on the medical certificate of the cause of death is inadequate, the coroner must be informed. ❞**

Recent developments

Two important government reviews have recently taken place. The third report of the Shipman Inquiry is now available, and the Review of Death Certification and Coroner Services was published in June 2003. Both recommend substantial changes to the procedure for registering deaths.

The recommendations differ in detail, but they are broadly similar.

They are currently being studied, and many of the recommendations are included in the draft bill on reform of the Coroner system, that was laid before parliament for scrutiny in June 2006.

It appears, nevertheless that recommendations for major changes in the process of death registration have not been included.

The registration procedure

The procedure for registering a death is a simple question-and-answer interview between the registrar and the informant.

The registrar will, first of all, make sure that the death took place in his or her sub-district; a death cannot be registered if it occurred in any place outside the registrar's sub-district. He or she will ask in what capacity whoever is registering the death qualifies to be the informant – relative, present at the death, or other reason.

Then the registrar fills in a draft form for the register of deaths with the date of death and exactly where it occurred, the sex, names and surname of the dead person. It is as well to give all the names by which the deceased has ever been known, so that there can be no doubt as to whom the particulars refer. In order to avoid difficulties over identity in connection with probate, insurance policies, pensions and bank accounts, the names should be the same as those on birth and marriage certificates, and on any other relevant documents. The date and place of birth of the dead person, and last address, are entered. For someone who died away from home, give the home address.

Next, the registrar will want to know the last full-time occupation of the deceased, and whether he or she was retired at the time of death.

A woman who was married or widowed at the time of her death would be described as 'wife of' or 'widow of', followed by the name and occupation of her husband, in addition to her own occupation or profession.

A woman who had never been married or a woman whose marriage had been dissolved would have her occupation recorded, with no reference to her marital status.

&& To avoid difficulties over identify, give all the names by which the deceased was known. ,,

 If you are registering a stillbirth, information is given on pages 56-7. For information on registering a death abroad or where to register if someone died on board an aircraft, see pages 58-9.

Population statistics

Additional information is required for the preparation of population statistics by the Registrar General. If the deceased was over 16 years old, additional information is requested: marital status at the time of death (single, married, widowed or divorced) and the date of birth of any widow or widower left. This information is not entered in the register in either England or Wales.

Children under the age of 16 are described as 'son of' or 'daughter of', followed by the names and occupations of the parents.

The registrar copies the medical cause of death from the doctor's certificate or the coroner's notification, and adds the name and qualification of the doctor or coroner.

On the draft form, but not in the register itself, the registrar enters the deceased's National Health Service number.

❝ The informant will have to sign the register, so be sure to check there is nothing wrong or misleading in the draft of the entry. ❞

ENTRY IN THE REGISTER

Many register offices are now computerised, so it is likely that your information about the deceased will be entered into a computer system and your copy, or copies, of the death certificate produced by a computer printer. Note that you, as informant, will still be required to sign the register in the usual way.

Check the draft of the proposed entry in the register to make sure that there is nothing wrong or misleading in it. When the particulars are agreed, the registrar makes the entry in the register itself and asks you to check and sign it. You should sign your usual signature. The registrar has to use special ink for the register, so sign with the pen offered. After adding the date of the registration, the registrar signs the entry in the final space.

Any errors can be corrected without formality before the entry has been signed, but once it is signed by the registrar, the entry cannot be corrected without documentary evidence to justify the correction. Some errors cannot be corrected without authorisation from the Registrar General.

The registrar can now let you have copies of the entry in the register (the death certificates). Three copies (each costs £3.50, 2006) should be sufficient, for:

- Obtaining probate or letters of administration (see pages 133–82)
- Dealing with the deceased's bank account
- Claims on insurance policies.

If you need advice on the number and type of certificates required, take a list of the purposes for which evidence of death may be required to the registrar, who will advise accordingly. New death certificates are printed on heavily watermarked paper, and photocopying these is a breach of copyright. However, individuals or organisations may take copies of death certificates for their own record-keeping purposes provided that the copies are not passed on to others as evidence of the death.

In addition to the copies of the death certificate, the registrar will provide, without charge, **Form BD8**

(see box, above) for Social Security purposes, and a **green certificate** for the funeral director or other person arranging the funeral, authorising the funeral to take place.

Obtaining death certificates at a later date

Further copies of death certificates may be obtained from the registrar who registered the death while the current volume of the death register remains in use. This is likely to be about one month, but the time varies according to how many deaths are registered each week and whether the death in question was entered near the beginning or end of the relevant register.

Make a note of the number of the entry in the register and the date, and also note down the registration district, because you may need more copies of the entry later.

When completed, each death register is passed to the Superintendent Registrar of the district, from whom copies of the death certificate may be obtained later if required. The charge for each certificate in this case is £7 (2006).

Applications for certificates by post or online can be made to the General Register Office (GRO – see below). The charge for this is £11.50 (2006) (or £10 online), but if the index number on a previously issued certificate is known and quoted, the fee is reduced to £8.50 (2006) if ordered by post, or £7 online. If all details of a previously issued certificate have been lost and the office where registration took place is not known, applications should be made to the Public Search Room in London (again, see below).

A priority service is available that enables certificates to be despatched the next working day following receipt of order. The charge in this case is £27.50 (£26 online), or, when full details are known, £24.50 if ordered by post, phone or fax, and £23 if ordered online.

With any postal application, send a stamped, addressed envelope, together with a cheque or postal order for the necessary amount. Applications by phone or online may be paid for by credit or debit card. When applying in person for a copy of a certificate, payment must be made at the time of application.

Registration in Scotland and Northern Ireland

For Scotland, see pages 60-4. In Northern Ireland, contact the Registrar General (Northern Ireland, see below). The charge for a standard death certificate is £11, with additional copies each costing £5.50. Certificates may be ordered by post, phone or online and will be supplied within three working days. There is an express service to obtain certificates within one hour; the charge for this is £27 but all applications must be received by 2.30pm (other than by applying in person) to be received on the next working day. This service is now available online (see also below). Those wishing to pay by credit card should telephone the special credit card line: 028 9025 2000.

Useful websites for obtaining death certificates at a later date are: www.gro.gov.uk (the General Register Office), www.groni.gov.uk (Registrar General, Northern Ireland) and www.gro-scotland.gov.uk (General Register Office, Scotland). To find out more about the Public Search Room, go to www.gro.gov.uk/pubsearch.asp.

> **"The certificate must be given to the funeral director, who will pass it on to the church, cemetery or crematorium officials. Without it, the body cannot be buried or cremated."**

ISSUE OF GREEN CERTIFICATE

The green certificate, sometimes referred to as the disposal certificate, that is given to you by the registrar authorises either burial or application for cremation. A body may not be buried or cremated without this certificate or its equivalent – the coroner's order for burial or certificate for cremation. It is unwise to make more than provisional arrangements for the funeral until you have the certificate from either the registrar or the coroner.

The registrar can issue this certificate before registering a death, but only when he or she has already received the requisite information (including medical evidence) and is just waiting for the informant to register the death – for instance, when the only suitable informant is ill in hospital but the funeral has to take place. A certificate issued by the registrar before registration authorises burial only; crematorium authorities are not allowed to accept such a certificate.

In certain circumstances, the coroner will issue the necessary documentation. If the death has been reported to the coroner and a post mortem examination has been ordered, only the coroner can authorise cremation; if the body is to be buried, the registrar can issue the burial certificate. If there has been an inquest, it is the coroner who issues either an **order for burial** or a **certificate for cremation**.

No fee is charged for a coroner's order. If you lose it, you (or the funeral director) have to apply for a duplicate to the coroner who issued the original certificate.

The funeral director's role

When you obtain the necessary certificate from the registrar or coroner, give it to the funeral director, who will take it to the church, cemetery or crematorium officials.

Without it, they will not bury or cremate a body. It is the responsibility of the church, cemetery or crematorium to complete Part C of the certificate and to return it to the registrar confirming disposal has taken place. If the registrar does not receive Part C within 14 days of the issue of the certificate, he or she will get in touch with the person to whom the certificate had been given.

Documents for registration

Document	Source	Function	Recipient
notice to informant	doctor	gives details of who must register death and what particulars will be required	via relative to registrar
medical certificate of cause of death	doctor	states cause of death	to registrar (direct or via relative)
If coroner involved: coroner's notification	coroner	confirms or gives details of cause of death	to registrar (direct or via relative)
or coroner's certificate after inquest	coroner	gives all the particulars required for death to be registered	direct to registrar

REGISTERING A STILLBIRTH

In the case of a stillbirth, both birth and death need to be registered, a single operation that has to be done within 42 days.

People qualified to register a stillbirth are (as for live births):

- The mother
- The father if the child would have been legitimate had it been born alive
- The occupier of the house or other premises in which the stillbirth occurred
- A person who was present at the stillbirth or who found the stillborn child.

A stillborn child is a child born after the 24th week of pregnancy which did not at any time after being completely delivered from its mother breathe or show any other signs of life. If a miscarriage occurs before the 24th week of pregnancy, it is legally regarded as a non-viable foetus, and there is no liability as to registration (see also pages 36–7).

If there is doubt about whether the child was born alive or not, the case must be reported to the coroner.

If a doctor was in attendance at a stillbirth or examined the body of the stillborn child, he or she can issue a certificate of stillbirth, stating the cause of stillbirth and the duration of the pregnancy. A certified midwife can also issue the certificate if no doctor was there. If no doctor or midwife was in attendance at, or after, the birth, one of the parents, or some other qualified informant, can make a declaration on a form (**Form 35**, available from the registrar of births and deaths), saying that to the best of his or her knowledge and belief the child was stillborn.

If there is any doubt whether the child was born alive or not, the case must be reported to the coroner of the district, who may then order a post mortem or an inquest and will issue a certificate of the cause of death when the inquiries are complete.

When registering a stillbirth, the registrar has to have the doctor's or midwife's certificate, or a declaration of the stillbirth. Whoever goes to register has to tell the registrar of:

- The name of the child where given
- The name, surname and maiden name of the mother
- Her place of birth and her usual residence at the time of the child's birth
- If she had never been married, her occupation is also required

- If the child would have been legitimate, the name, surname and occupation of the father and his place of birth.

If the father and mother are married to each other, the registrar asks the month and year of the marriage, and the number of the mother's previous children, both born alive and stillborn, by her present and any former husband; this information is needed for statistical purposes only and is not entered in the register.

If the parents are not married at the time of their baby's birth but do still want the father's details entered, they should ask the registrar to guide them through the rather more involved procedures.

A certified copy of the stillbirth entry (death certificate) is now obtainable, costing £3.50, although a certificate of registration will be provided free of charge to the informant if it is requested. If additional copies are required at a later date, the GRO must be contacted by phone or in writing by the mother or father (if he is named on the certificate). The cost for these is £7 (2006). A special application form must be completed.

Recent Developments

Two important government reviews have recently taken place. The third report of the Shipman Inquiry is now available, and the Review of Death Certification and Coroner Services was published in June 2003. Both recommend substantial changes to the procedure for registering deaths. The recommendations differ in detail, but are broadly similar. They are currently being studied, and have not been implemented to date. Indeed, it does not seem likely that they will be put in place in the immediate future. However, it is possible that eventually registration of death will be dealt with by a reformed and expanded Coroner's Service.

❝ Government reviews have recommended major changes to how deaths are registered. It may eventually be handled by a reformed and expanded Coroner's Service. ❞

Research shows that bereaved parents often mourn the death of their child far longer than a widow or widower mouns the death of their spouse. To read about the grief process, see pages 38–44.

REGISTERING A DEATH ABROAD

When a British subject dies abroad, whether as a resident or as a visitor, the death must be registered where he or she died according to local regulations and customs. This is far from uncommon: in recent years, more than 2,000 British deaths abroad have been reported annually to the Foreign Office. In many countries, the British consul can also register the death: this has the advantage that certified copies of the entry in the Register of Deaths can eventually be obtained from the General Register Office (www.gro.gov.uk), just as if the death had been registered in the UK.

If it is required that the death be recorded in the consular register in order to make records of the death available in the UK, the next of kin or executor should obtain, complete and return an application form to the Nationality and Passport Section of the Foreign and Commonwealth Office (FCO), together with the death certificate issued by the local authorities in the country concerned.

- If the consular office in the country where the death occurred is aware of the death, a separate document bearing a consular stamp is usually included with the package of documents accompanying the body. This document should also be sent to the Nationality and Passport Section of the FCO with the application form.
- If the consular office where the death took place is not aware of the death, then the passport and birth certificate should be sent with the application as proof of UK citizenship; these will be returned to the applicant.

Fees payable

A consular fee is payable for the registration of the death in the UK, and a further fee is payable for each certificate issued at the time of registration; these fees vary periodically, and applicants should ask the FCO what fees are needed to accompany their application. This is a lengthy process, and considerable delay should be expected.

❝When someone dies in an aircraft, the death must be registered in the country to which the aircraft belongs.❞

 To get in touch with the Foreign and Commonwealth Office, go to www.fco.gov.uk and key in 'death abroad' into the Quick Search box. There is lots of advice and plenty of links to other helpful agencies.

If such application is not made, there will be no official record of the death in the UK. In this case, in order for the funeral to take place, the registrar of the relevant district must be asked to supply a registrar's certificate confirming that the death is not required to be registered, commonly called a '**certificate of no liability to register**'. For this, a copy of the foreign death certificate, suitably translated into English (although many European countries now use a multi-lingual death certificate, which does not need translation), must be supplied, giving the cause of death. The funeral director will normally be able to obtain both the translation and the certificate. Consular registration can take place after the funeral: a 'certificate of no liability to register' does not inhibit this process.

REGISTERING A DEATH IN THE AIR

When death occurs in an aircraft, the death must be registered in the country to which that aircraft belongs. At the next landing following the death, the captain must notify the local police authorities and the appropriate registration authority, which may not be in the same country as the one where the aircraft has landed. Subsequent action concerning arrangements for the body varies according to local regulations, but as far as relatives are concerned, the procedure is the same as that for a death that occurs abroad (see page 99–100). These arrangements can be extremely complicated, and will normally be dealt with by the funeral director in conjunction with a specialist repatriation service.

Registration in Scotland

The medical certificate of the cause of death given by doctors in Scotland is similar to that in England. The obligation to give the certificate rests on the doctor who attended the deceased during the last illness, but, if there was no doctor in attendance, the certificate may be issued by any doctor who is able to do so.

The doctor hands the certificate to a relative to take to the local registrar or sends it direct to the registrar. In the majority of cases, the certificate is issued to a relative.

If a medical certificate of cause of death cannot be given, the registrar can, nevertheless, register the death but must report the facts of the case to the procurator fiscal.

“There must be a public inquiry into deaths in legal custody or from work accidents. These are heard in the local sheriff court, and it is the sheriff who determines the circumstances of the death. ”

THE PROCURATOR FISCAL

There are no coroners in Scotland and the duties which in England would be carried out by a coroner, are in Scotland carried out by a procurator fiscal (a full-time law officer, who comes under the authority of the Lord Advocate).

The procurator fiscal has many functions, including responsibility for investigating all sudden, unexpected and violent deaths and also any death that occurred under suspicious circumstances. If satisfied with the doctor's medical certificate and any evidence received from the police, he or she need take no further action. If, however, the procurator fiscal considers a further medical report is necessary, a medical practitioner (frequently a police surgeon) will be requested to report 'on soul and conscience' what he or she considers was the cause of death.

Post mortem

The procurator fiscal will decide whether or not a post mortem is necessary. In the majority of cases, a post mortem is not carried out and the doctor certifies the cause of death after an external examination. The mere fact that the cause of death is, in a medical sense, unexplained is not a ground for ordering a dissection at public expense, provided the intrinsic circumstances explain sufficiently the cause of death in a popular sense and do not raise a suspicion of criminality or negligence.

If a post mortem is carried out, one doctor is usually sufficient but if, while conducting the dissection, the doctor finds unexpected difficulties, the procurator fiscal may decide to bring in a second doctor. Where there is a possibility of criminal proceedings being taken against someone and it is necessary to prove the fact and cause of death, or where the death is drugs-related, a post mortem should be carried out by two medical practitioners.

PUBLIC INQUIRY

Death while in legal custody or as the result of an accident during work must be the subject of a public inquiry (called a Fatal Accident Inquiry or FAI), which takes the place of an inquest in England. If a person, while engaged in industrial employment or occupation, died of natural causes, there may, but will not necessarily, be a public inquiry.

A public inquiry is heard before the sheriff in the local sheriff court. The procurator fiscal and the representatives of any other interested parties examine the witnesses but it is the sheriff who determines the circumstances of the death.

The procurator fiscal has to report certain cases to the Crown Office (see box on page 62) and it is the Lord Advocate who makes the final decision about whether to apply to a sheriff for an inquiry to be held. In all other cases, investigations made into sudden deaths are carried out by the procurator fiscal confidentially. Before reporting a case to the Crown Office, the procurator fiscal may interview witnesses and the relatives in private (this is called a precognition).

The information that is given on these pages only concerns subjects that are treated differently in Scotland to England and Wales. For all other information, please read the main sections in the book.

Crown Office cases

Cases that are reported to the Crown Office because they may result in a public inquiry are essentially those involving a matter of the public interest – for instance, to prevent a recurrence of similar circumstances. Deaths that are directly or indirectly connected with the action of a third party, such as road traffic deaths, may be reported to the Crown Office for consideration either of criminal proceedings or of a public inquiry.

REGISTERING THE DEATH

In Scotland, the law requires that every death must be registered within eight days from the date of death.

The person qualified to act as informant for registering a death is:

- Any relative of the deceased
- Any person present at the death
- The deceased's executor or other legal representative
- The occupier of the premises where the death took place
- Or any person having knowledge of the particulars to be registered.

Whereas in England a death must be registered in the registration office for the district in which the death occurred, in Scotland the death may be registered either in the office for the district in which the death occurred or in the office for the district in which the deceased had normally resided before the death, provided this was also in Scotland. The death of a visitor to Scotland must be registered where the death took place.

As in England, the procedure for registering a death is a simple question-and-answer interview between registrar and informant. The registrar will request the production of a medical certificate of cause of death

"In Scotland deaths can be registered in the district where death occurred, or where the deceased normally resided. "

See pages 50-2 for an overview of what happens at the registrar's office and page 48 for a list of what information will be required by the registrar.

or, failing that, the name and address of a doctor who can be asked to give the certificate. The information required by a Scottish registrar to register a death is much the same as in England and Wales (see page 48), except that he or she also needs to know the time of death; if the deceased had ever been married, the name, surname and occupation of each spouse and date of birth of the surviving spouse; and the name and occupation of the deceased's father and the name, occupation and maiden name of the mother, and whether the parents are alive or dead.

Having said that, in most cases, if one or two of these additional items of information are not known, then registration of the death can usually proceed without the information. But it is always better to produce this information for the registrar where at all possible in order not to delay the process.

Registering a stillbirth

A stillbirth in Scotland must be registered within 21 days and can be registered either in the district in which it took place or in the district in Scotland in which the mother of the stillborn child was ordinarily resident at the time of the stillbirth. As in England, if no doctor or midwife can issue a certificate of stillbirth, an informant must make a declaration on a special form. In Scotland this is **Form 7**, obtainable from the registrar. All such cases, and any case where there is doubt as to whether the child was alive or not, are reported to the procurator fiscal, who notifies the Registrar General of the results of his or her investigations.

If the body is to be cremated, a certificate of stillbirth must be given by the doctor who was in attendance at the confinement (or who conducted the post mortem). The stillbirth must

> **❝ A certificate of stillbirth must be given by the doctor who was in attendance. The stillbirth must be registered before cremation. ❞**

 The subject of grieving over the loss of a baby is also discussed on pages 38-44 together with what help you can get if you feel you need counselling to help with your bereavement.

be registered before cremation can take place.

The informant must produce for the registrar a doctor's or midwife's certificate, or the completed Form 7, and is required to give the same information as in England and, in addition, the time of the stillbirth and, where applicable, the place of the parents' marriage.

CERTIFICATE OF REGISTRATION

There is no direct equivalent in Scotland of a green certificate. After registration, the registrar issues to the informant a certificate of registration of death (**Form 14**), which should be given to the funeral director to give to the keeper of the burial ground or to the crematorium authorities. There is no charge for this certificate.

DEATH CERTIFICATES

As in England, the registrar also issues, free of charge, a registration or notification of death form, which can be used for National Insurance and Social Security purposes. All other death certificates must be paid for.

Death certificates (a full copy of an entry in the death register, sometimes called an extract) are always obtainable from the registrar of the district where the death was registered and cost £8.50 at the time of registration and £13.50 if obtained outside the year of registration.

❝ Death certificates (sometimes called an extract) are obtainable from the registrar of the district where the death was registered. ❞

Funeral arrangements

When someone dies, many people want to 'get the funeral over with as soon as possible'; it is wise, however, to allow enough time to recover from the shock of the first 48 hours, and plan a funeral that will be an appropriate memorial to the person who has passed away.

The funeral director

Sometimes the deceased will leave specific requests about his or her funeral in the will – see page 143 for obtaining a will. If the deceased left no specific instructions, however, the decision about burial or cremation is normally made by the next of kin, or the executor.

William Russell, the first undertaker in the UK, began business in London in 1680; he was succeeded by carpenters who specialised in producing coffins and carriage proprietors who developed special funeral carriages. These functions merged, and a profession of men who 'undertook' to provide a funeral service arose. The Victorian era saw the popularisation of elaborate, often ostentatious, and usually expensive funerals.

Undertakers are now known as funeral directors and the vast majority of them now belong to one of two associations:

- **The National Association of Funeral Directors** (NAFD)
- Or the **National Society of Allied and Independent Funeral Directors** (SAIF)

(Since January 2004, the NAFD incorporates the former Funeral Standards Council (FSC) after its members voted to amalgamate with the NAFD.)

You should be sure to choose a funeral director who is affiliated to one of these organisations – if the firm is unregistered, you might have no form of redress in the event of any problems. The NAFD has a Code of Practice, which includes providing information about services and prices, a written estimate of charges and a

❝ It is still rare for a funeral to be carried out without the services of a funeral director. ❞

The websites for the two funeral director associations are: www.nafd.org.uk (NAFD) and www.saif.org.uk. For information about funerals and bereavement, including finding your nearest funeral director, go to www.uk-funerals.co.uk.

detailed funeral account. Members must offer a basic funeral if requested to do so. The code covers general and professional conduct, including confidentiality and a procedure for complaints. SAIF has a similar Code of Practice and complaints procedure. Under the code, drawn up in consultation with the Office of Fair Trading (OFT), SAIF members are required to refrain from offensive or aggressive marketing techniques; this also applies to the selling of pre-paid funeral plans.

The Funeral Ombudsman Scheme is unfortunately no longer operative. However, both of the funeral trade organisations give access to a complaints and arbitration process for those people who are unable to resolve any problems or complaints with their local funeral director.

Funeral directors and the government

The Office of Fair Trading (OFT) commenced an inquiry into the funerals business in March 2000, and published a report in July 2001. In preparing the report, views were invited from the funeral trade and other interested parties including burial and cremation organisations, bereavement and counselling groups,

❝ Choose a funeral director who is a member of one of the trade bodies, both of which have a complaints and arbitration process. ❞

local authorities, NHS trusts, and consumer and community representatives. The number of submissions received was 188. This was complemented by a survey of 400 individuals with recent experience of arranging a funeral, and a survey of funeral directors, which produced approximately 2,000 responses.

The surveys revealed that the great majority of those arranging funerals were content, with 96 per cent of respondents saying that they were satisfied or very satisfied. The number of complaints reported to official sources was very low, and funeral directors were generally perceived to be sensitive, flexible and patient.

 The website of the Office of Fair Trading is www.oft.gov.uk. Key in the words 'funerals business' into the search box and you will be given the link to the report made by the OFT in July 2001.

However, the report found that compliance with published Codes of Practice was often patchy; people were still failing to receive price lists, clear written estimates of the cost of a funeral, or details of the basic funeral service. The report stopped short of recommending new legislation for the regulation of the funeral business, but instead pushed strongly for the trade associations to seek OFT approval for robust Codes of Practice under a new initiative promoting such codes.

An increasing number of funeral directors have qualified counsellors offering bereavement care.

In February 2003, the OFT launched its consumer codes approval scheme to UK business with the result that a number of recommendations were made:

- **Price lists** should be prominently displayed and made available for people to take away
- **Written estimates** and invoices should be provided for all transactions
- **Written estimates** should be given out during the initial interview, when available services are first discussed; clients should then be asked if they wish to proceed
- **Every funeral outlet** should prominently display details of the organisation that has ultimate control of the business
- **When funeral directors operate contracts** for the coroner, they should not seek to influence an individual's choice of funeral director
- **The funeral trade associations** (the NAFD and SAIF) should seek to obtain OFT approval for Codes of Practice under the OFT's new approach to such codes
- **Funeral businesses that offer credit** should comply with the Consumer Credit Act 1974 and the various consumer credit regulations
- **Literature** produced by local authorities, NHS trusts, cemeteries and crematoria should be made more widely available in places that those arranging funerals are likely to visit.

The OFT, in partnership with the National Funerals College, makes a template available to those publishing advice on funerals (particularly local authorities and NHS trusts) which sets out information for people on the practical aspects of arranging a funeral.

 To find out more about the OFT and funerals, go to www.oft.gov.uk/Consumer/Your+Rights+When+Shopping/Funerals/default.htm.

The OFT also encourages local directories, such as *Thomson Local* and *Yellow Pages*, to publish succinct guidance for people, in order to ensure that information is available prior to the making of funeral arrangements. Further information should be available in register offices, libraries, doctors' surgeries, hospitals and nursing homes.

Funeral directors and their clients

The funeral director's purpose is to assume total responsibility for organising and supplying all that is needed for a funeral, and to provide as much care as possible for the grieving relatives. In many cases, the member of staff with whom you have the first interview will remain in charge until after the funeral is completed. Some clients want the funeral director to do everything for them, and have no wish to be directly involved in the funeral. Others want to be involved as much as possible: they may carefully think out a funeral service, select music and readings, arrange for family bearers to carry the coffin, have a member of the family give an address, and so on. It is the responsibility of the funeral director to do his or her best to carry out the client's wishes, and to assist the client with any practical participation chosen.

A small but growing number of funeral directors are now offering bereavement care services, with qualified counsellors on the staff. All should be able to refer clients to bereavement care organisations, where this is necessary. Nevertheless, the arrangement of a funeral is a business transaction and should be treated as such; it is often difficult for bereaved relatives to be businesslike in the circumstances, but most funeral directors are understanding and will give all the assistance needed. The family or friends of the deceased person should agree who is to be in charge of supervising the arrangements, and must recognise that the person who ultimately takes responsibility for the funeral arrangements is also responsible for seeing that the bill is paid (but see also below). It is not part of an executor's formal duty to arrange the funeral when someone has died, although it is a responsibility often taken on.

 It's a good idea to agree the form and costs of the funeral with co-executors and family members to ensure what you have in mind is acceptable.

 When it comes to paying the bill for the funeral, while you are responsible for seeing that it is paid, the actual cost can come out of the deceased's estate - see pages 141 and 185.

The cost of a funeral

It is natural to want to give the deceased person a good send off but it is also important to keep the potential costs in mind. It is easy to ask your funeral director, if you are using one, to arrange this, that and the other, but ensure you keep track of how everything might add up.

At the time of arranging the funeral, you should have a fairly clear idea of the kind of funeral that is wanted, and approximately how much money should be spent on it. Many people have no real idea of how much funerals are likely to cost.

Until recently, the Oddfellows Friendly Society published an annual survey of funeral costs, the last of which took place in 2000, after which the society was acquired by American Life. American Life have commissioned a survey for 2006,

carried out by Gilmour Research in the autumn of 2005. There is no certainty that the current findings are as accurate as those published by Oddfellows; nevertheless, they give a good indication of the way in which funeral costs have changed.

In 2000, the average cost of a simple cremation funeral in England, Wales and Scotland was £1,214; by 2006 this had risen to £1,954. There are considerable regional differences in costs: the cheapest average was in the North West at £1,784, while the dearest average was the West Midlands at £2,265. Ipswich was found to provide the cheapest cremation at £1,373 and Luton the most expensive at £3,200.

Similarly, while in 2000 the average cost of a funeral involving burial was £2,048, the 2006 equivalent amounted to £3,307. There continue to be significant regional differences with regard to burial costs – a funeral including burial costs an average of £5,753 in London compared with an average of £2,480 in the East

“Many people are unaware that the average cost of a simple cremation funeral is £1,954, while for a burial it is £3,307. There are significant regional differences in these prices, and the cost of burial rises about a tenth per year. ”

Midlands, with Manchester providing the cheapest burial at £1,797 and Southgate, London, the most expensive at £6,140. All these costs related to a simple funeral with no frills or extras provided. This means the cost of burials is rising by approximately 10 per cent per annum, while cremation costs are slightly lower at 8 per cent per annum.

Members of both the NAFD and SAIF require their members to provide printed price lists and written estimates.

Some people find the expenses of a funeral very difficult to meet, and are embarrassed about telling the funeral director. In fact, one of the first things a funeral director should do is to find out whether or not there is a problem about money and, if there is, advise the client of ways in which help may be provided.

All members of both trade organisations are pledged to provide a basic funeral. This may be given a different title by different funeral directors, but it will provide:

- The removal and care of the deceased during normal office hours within a limited locality
- The arrangement of a basic funeral
- The provision of a hearse only and staff to the nearest crematorium or cemetery
- The provision of a basic coffin
- No chapel visits (although such

 The funeral director can provide quotations for anything from a simple, basic funeral at minimal price to elaborate arrangements costing a great deal of money. In all cases, he or she should provide a written estimate of the cost of the proposed funeral and, when the estimate has been given, ask whether the client wishes to proceed.

visits are generally permitted during office hours)
- The conducting of the funeral at a time suitable to the funeral directors.

This will be provided at an inclusive package price, which is significantly lower than standard charges, and many funeral directors will go well beyond the minimum requirements when supplying a basic funeral.

Normally, the cost of the funeral is paid for from the estate of the deceased – the money and property that has been left. Banks will normally release funds to pay for the funeral from the bank account of the deceased, if they are presented with an itemised account from the funeral director and a copy of the death certificate.

FUNERAL DIRECTOR FEES

Funeral directors are in business, and will bring to the notice of clients all the various services on offer, including a range of coffins and caskets, the provision of flowers for the funeral, placing obituary notices in the local and national press, providing printed service sheets, laying on catering for family gatherings after the funeral, and providing special music such as a trumpeter, piper, or even a New Orleans jazz band. Reputable funeral directors will bring various alternatives to your attention without attempting to get you to pay for something you do not want, but do not be pressurised into signing up for something against your better judgement.

You can make preliminary arrangements with a funeral director on the telephone, but to make full arrangements for the funeral it will be necessary either for him or her to come to your home, or for you to make an appointment to visit the office. There are matters to be explained and papers to be signed: in the case of cremation, statutory documents must be signed by the client and the signature countersigned by an independent witness who is also a householder – someone not living in rented accommodation – before the funeral can take place. In practice, the funeral director making the arrangement with the client is usually acceptable as an independent witness provided he or she is a householder.

The funeral director must show you the price list for all the funerals and services he or she can provide. You can ask for this in advance, and discuss the alternatives with other members of the family or friends. If you are contacting several funeral directors, be sure you are comparing like with like: ask for printed price lists, not just verbal estimates, and be very suspicious if none are available. Find out what is included in the inclusive prices, and visit the funeral director's premises if at all possible – you can do this without any commitment. You will gain a far better idea of the services available than by making a telephone call. Not only may the prices charged vary considerably, but so may the quality and condition of vehicles, chapels of rest and so on. No funeral director should object to showing you what he or she can provide.

> **" Ask for printed price costs so that you are comparing like with like. Visiting the premises will give you a far better idea of the services that are available than making a phone call. "**

Funeral estimates

The estimate for the funeral account will be in two parts:

- **Fees that the funeral director will charge you for his or her services:** for collecting the body of the deceased; caring for the deceased person until the funeral; arranging and conducting the funeral; and supplying the hearse, limousine, staff and so on.
- **Fees that the funeral director will pay to third parties (disbursements)** for services supplied on your behalf, such as:
  - doctors' fees for cremation papers
  - crematorium or burial fees
  - fees for the church, minister, organist, gravediggers, obituaries, flowers and so on.

The funeral director will pay for all or most of the disbursements in advance and will usually add the relevant amounts to the funeral account, to be paid after the funeral. However, an increasing number of funeral directors ask their clients to pay for disbursements in advance, usually at the time of the funeral arrangement.

Many funeral directors make no charge, or only a nominal charge, for the funerals of babies and small children; some will extend this courtesy to funerals for children up to school-leaving age. The funeral director will have little option, however, but to pass on fees or disbursements that may be charged by churches, crematoria or burial authorities.

When funeral arrangements have been made to your satisfaction, you will often be asked to sign the arrangement form as a contractual agreement that the funeral director will supply the services specified and that you will, according to the funeral director's terms and conditions, in due course pay for them.

> ## VAT
>
> The services of the funeral director, minister and cemetery or crematorium are exempt from VAT. If, however, the funeral director supplies flowers, catering or any form of memorial, the VAT must be paid on these items.

It should always be remembered that the person who takes responsibility for arranging the funeral also becomes responsible for ensuring that the funeral account is paid.

For information about help on paying for funeral costs, see pages 77–8. You can also pay for your funeral in advance, which is discussed on page 78.

Burial or cremation?

The choice of cremation rather than burial may involve many different factors, but as far as cost is concerned, cremation is usually cheaper – sometimes much cheaper. Charges vary around the country, but an average cost of £350 to £450 for cremation must be set against an average cost of £400 to £600 for burial of a local resident in a municipal cemetery.

Ancillary fees of £124 for doctors' cremation papers set against anything up to £300 for gravediggers' fees (when not included in the charges of the cemetery authority) weight the difference even more. Fees for burial in some country cemeteries are often considerably cheaper for local residents; fees for non-residents, where they are accepted for burial, may be doubled, and sometimes tripled or quadrupled. Burial in Church of England churchyards is usually cheaper than in a municipal or private cemetery; the fees for 2006 were £247 (£87 for the funeral service in church and £160 for the following burial in the churchyard, to which the cost of digging the grave must be added). But most churchyards have little, if any, grave space left, and can accommodate only the burial of ashes caskets in small plots, or arrange for a second interment in a double-depth grave.

The fees for the funeral services of the Church of England churches and clergy are set annually by the Archbishops' Council, and are followed by most other denominations. The fixed annual fees are divided into two parts, one part to the parochial church council (PCC), which includes the service of the church building and verger, and the other part going towards the provision of the incumbent's salary. Extra costs for heating and use of the organ, etc. will sometimes be added; these fees will be the same for burial as for cremation.

The Church of England will charge the same fee for a minister's services (£87 in 2006) if the funeral takes place at a crematorium chapel, or anywhere other than the church of which he or she is the incumbent. In central areas of large cities, burial fees may increase to many hundreds – sometimes thousands – of pounds.

The growing shortage of space for burials in existing cemeteries and the difficulties incurred in providing new cemeteries inevitably mean that there can be considerable

 For information on specific costs relating to cremations, see page 84; and for burials, see page 94.

increases in costs. Many cemetery authorities do not provide the services of a gravedigger, in which case costs will be incurred as mentioned above.

Coffins

Some funeral directors charge for a complete service, including a coffin, while others break their costs down into charges for vehicles, professional services and so on, and charge separately for the client's choice of coffin.

In the case of an inclusive funeral service, the choice of a more expensive type of coffin usually provides a more elaborate type of funeral. Your funeral director should be able to show you examples or illustrations of the different coffins and caskets that he or she can supply for a funeral.

The material from which a coffin is made greatly affects the price:

- **The most basic type** of coffin will be made from chipboard laminated with plastic foil
- **A standard type** from wood-veneered chipboard or MDF (medium density fibreboard)
- **A superior coffin** or casket from solid wood, such as mahogany or ash.
- **Cardboard coffins** are now readily available, and are often chosen by families who want to paint or otherwise decorate their coffin.

- **Woven coffins** made from wicker, willow or bamboo are increasing in popularity, and are often chosen by those who feel strongly about environmental issues. It is advisable to inspect all coffins before deciding on a purchase.

There is little variation in the cost of coffin linings and fittings, although if solid brass handles are requested, these will be expensive. Remember to notify the funeral director if the coffin should or should not bear a (Christian) cross. For cremation, metal fittings are inadmissible; handles and

 It is worth remembering that the coffins offered for simple, basic funerals are intended for cremation rather than burial. To keep costs and prices down, the coffin is constructed to be suitable for carrying into a crematorium and placing on the catafalque but may not be sturdy enough to withstand the rigours of being lowered into a grave. It is advisable to choose a more sturdily constructed coffin if burial is envisaged; this does *not* mean buying the most expensive coffin – the funeral director will advise accordingly.

fittings are made of plastic which has been electroplated with brass or nickel. Indeed, there are rigid by-laws which control the materials used in the construction of coffins for cremation. For each cremation, the funeral director must sign that he or she has conformed to the government's and the crematorium's requirements.

Some funeral directors buy plain coffins, which are then lined and fitted with handles according to their client's choice; others offer their clients a variety of coffins already fitted and lined.

Each coffin must be fitted with a nameplate that contains the name of the deceased; it is normal for the plate also to contain the date of death and the deceased's age.

> **❝Even though some people don't want to be involved in many practical decisions about the funeral, they should be given a written estimate of the costs, although these may change. ❞**

Other costs

It must be remembered that the total cost of the funeral will consist of the fees the funeral director will charge for his or her professional services, the fees paid to other agencies on behalf of the client, and any special services that are required beyond those supplied in the standard funeral package (such as the removal of a body from a house or nursing home out of standard working hours, additional limousines, and a charge for mileage if the funeral involves travelling some considerable distance). There will also be an extra charge if the body is to be taken into church on the evening before the funeral, or for supplying a casket for the burial of cremated remains (ashes).

The funeral director should give an itemised written estimate of the costs and a formal confirmation of funeral arrangements. Some people may feel that they do not want to be involved in too many practical decisions about the funeral, and want to leave it to the funeral director; it is still important for them to be given a written estimate of the cost. The estimate may well be amended as the bereaved relatives discuss the developing funeral arrangements, and decide on changes, such as the placement of obituaries, or an extra limousine, or indeed reduce the bill by removing various items from the funeral arrangement. The estimate is a clear outline of what the funeral is likely to cost, but is *not* the bill: the funeral director will submit the account shortly after the funeral takes place.

Funeral directors will explain the charges and conditions made for different churches in the local area, and the different fees charged by cemeteries and crematoria.

- **Nonconformist churches** such as the Methodist, Baptist and United Reformed Churches do not usually set fees for funerals, but tend to accept the same fees as those laid down by the Church of England (see page 94). Fees for the funeral of a member of the church or congregation are frequently waived. Such churches do not usually have graveyards, although there are exceptions: church funeral services are usually followed by cremation, or burial in a local cemetery.
- **Roman Catholic churches** do not set fees for funeral services either, but will accept a gift towards the ministry of the church. Sometimes this is taken care of by the family of the deceased person, but more usually the funeral director will provide a gift commensurate with the fees paid to the Church of England.

HELP WITH FUNERAL EXPENSES

If you do not have enough money to pay for the funeral, and you or your partner are getting Income Support, income-based Jobseeker's Allowance, Pension Credit, Housing Benefit, Child Tax Credit (at a rate higher than the family element), Working Tax Credit (where a disabled worker is included in the assessment) or Council Tax Benefit, you may be able to get a Funeral Payment from the Social Fund to help with the cost. The decision is based on *your* financial circumstances, not those of the person who died. If you qualify for a payment from the Social Fund, your savings are no longer taken into consideration. For more information, see leaflet SB16 *A Guide to the Social Fund*, which is available from your local Jobcentre plus office.

A number of local authorities now provide a municipal funeral service. This is done by contracting with local funeral directors for the provision of simple, low-cost funerals for residents of the local authority area. The London boroughs of Lambeth and Lewisham operate such a scheme, and a similar one exists in Cardiff. The cost is considerably less than that of an average local funeral.

 There are other state benefits that are available on the death of a spouse or close relative, such as bereavement benefits, income support and housing tax and council tax benefit. For more information see pages 199-203.

Paying for a funeral in advance

While in terms of purchasing power, the cost of a funeral is less than half what it was 70 years ago, a funeral still costs a considerable amount of money. Some people who have had to pay for the funerals of relatives and friends have found it difficult to find the money to pay the bill, and have decided that they want to pay for their own funeral in advance. For some, this is not only to spare relatives from facing the cost of their funeral, but because they want to specify how things are to be done, and what they would like to take place at their own funeral. To find out more, contact the following:

Age Concern: Tel: 0800 731 0651,
www.ageconcern.org.uk

Co-operative Funeral Care: Tel: 0800 289120,
www.co-operativefuneralcare.co.uk

Cruse Bereavement Care: Tel: 020 8939 9530,
www.crusebereavementcare.org.uk

Dignity Funeral Plans: Tel: 01942 799810,
www.funeral-plans-uk.co.uk

Golden Charter Funeral Plans: Tel: 0800 833800,
www.golden-charter.co.uk

Golden Leaves Funeral Plan: Tel: 0800 854448,
www.goldenleaves.co.uk

Help the Aged: Tel: 020 7278 1114,
www.helptheaged.org.uk

Perfect Assurance Funeral Trust (NAFD): Tel: 0121 709 0019, www.nafd.org.uk

Relatives of a member of the armed forces who dies in service may receive help with funeral costs from the Ministry of Defence (see page 103).

When someone without relatives dies, and no one can be found to pay for the funeral, the local district council where the person died (or hospital, if the death occurred in hospital) is responsible for arranging the funeral and paying for the cost. If the police have a body in their charge for which no relative can be traced, they notify the local authority, which will then provide a minimum-price funeral. Many hospitals have a 'funeral fund' and most local authorities have contracts with local funeral directors for the provision of such funerals. Arrangements vary considerably in different areas. If the provision of such a funeral is likely to be needed, acquaintances of the deceased must not approach any funeral director to begin making funeral arrangements. If they do, responsibility for funeral costs will then fall upon them, as local authorities have no power to reimburse costs where a third party has already made funeral arrangements. The local authority may recoup the cost of the funeral from the estate of the deceased, or from anyone who was responsible for maintaining the deceased while still alive.

Most funeral directors are sympathetic to clients with little money who have to arrange a funeral but do not meet the criteria for a grant from the Social Fund. The majority will provide a basic funeral at minimum cost; it is sometimes possible to spread this cost over a number of monthly payments. The funeral director should be told at the outset if there are financial difficulties, and ways will usually be found to give practical assistance.

Cremation arrangements

At the time of writing, more than 70 per cent of funerals involve cremation. The high proportion of cremations is partly due to the fact that cremation is almost always cheaper than burial. There has also been a radical shift in attitudes, which has developed since cremation began to be popular in the early years of the last century. This section describes the forms that need to be gathered together before a cremation and a breakdown of the costs that are involved.

There are about 240 crematoria in the UK, most of which are operated by municipal authorities, although private companies own a small proportion. Each crematorium has its own scale of fees, which usually increase annually; there is considerable variation in fees, but nothing like the great disparity that occurs in burial fees. Most crematoria publish brochures giving details of their services and fees, and most organise open days, usually on a Sunday, when the general public can investigate the whole cremation procedure. Most crematoria are open during office hours from Monday to

Mercury emissions from crematoria

Mercury vapour is emitted by crematoria from dental fillings, which contain mercury amalgam. Under certain conditions, this inorganic mercury transforms into organic compounds, which fall as rain and affect the food chain, especially sea food. This has a detrimental effect on the human body, which cannot get rid of mercury once it has been absorbed. The cumulative effect of this has caused concern to several governments. As a result, DEFRA has required all British crematoria to reduce mercury emissions by 50% by 1 January 2012. Some crematoria will filtrate 100% of their cremations, while others will not be able to filtrate at all due to the expense, but would, through a scheme called the Cremation Abatement of Mercury Emissions Organisation (CAMEO), contribute towards the costs of those that did. The process will be monitored to ensure an overall national filtration level of at least 50%. This will inevitably mean that the cost of cremation funerals will rise.

Friday, although some open on a Saturday morning. A number will offer cremation outside normal working hours at an extra charge, which is usually quite considerable. Almost all will have a 'garden of remembrance', landscaped grounds in which the cremated remains (ashes) of the deceased can be scattered or buried following a cremation funeral.

When the government brought in the Environmental Protection Act in 1990, many crematoria had to install new, more efficient cremators in order to conform with the regulations regarding pollution and the environment. This has been an enormously expensive operation, and the charges set by most crematoria have risen considerably in recent years as a result. The necessary systems to filtrate mercury emissions will lead to further price rises.

THE FORMALITIES

Before cremation can take place, the cause of death has to be established beyond any reasonable doubt. Should any question arise concerning the cause of death after a burial, an exhumation and pathological examination can take place; this is obviously not possible following a

Documents required for cremation

When death is due to natural causes and the coroner is not involved, the following forms have to be completed before cremation can take place. The first form must be completed by the next of kin or the executor, and the others by three different doctors. These forms are issued by the local crematorium; funeral directors keep a supply, and doctors usually keep a supply of those relevant to them.

The forms required are:
- Medical certificate of the cause of death (issued by the deceased's doctor to the next of kin)
- Registrar's certificate for burial or cremation (the green certificate issued by the registrar following registration)
- Form A (the application for cremation)
- Form to authorise the disposal of the cremated remains (ashes): usually reverse of Form A
- Service details form (gives the crematorium details of the funeral service to take place)
- Form B (signed by the deceased's GP or hospital consultant)
- Form C (signed by an independent doctor)
- Form F (signed by the local medical referee after scrutiny of Forms B and C).

cremation. If the deceased's doctor knows the cause of death beyond any reasonable doubt, he or she will sign the medical certificate of the cause of death, which, when given to the next of kin, will enable the death to be registered. If the funeral is to involve cremation, however, the doctor must also carry out an examination and complete a certificate of examination (**Form B**), which must be corroborated by a second doctor on a similar form (**Form C**) (see below).

Form A

This is the application for cremation, and has to be completed by the next of kin or the executor, and countersigned by a householder who knows him or her personally. In most situations, the funeral director will be acceptable as counter-signatory, but some crematoria insist on someone else signing the form. A revision of **Form A** was introduced in the Cremation (Amendment) Regulations 2006. This included civil partnerships as a recognised category of applicant in addition to those married or unmarried, widow or widower.

Forms B and C

These certificates of examination are on the same piece of paper, which often includes **Form F** (see page 82) as well.

Form B has to be completed by the doctor who attended the deceased during the last illness and must have been qualified for at least five years. He or she must examine the body

Pacemaker removal

Should a doctor be required to remove a cardiac pacemaker (which is essential if cremation is to take place), a fee for this will be a matter for negotiation between the doctor and the local Primary Care Trust. This removal, however, may be carried out by the funeral director's staff as part of his or her inclusive charges.

before the form can be completed. This may or may not be the patient's normal GP. The doctor may have to ask the relatives or acquaintances for some of the information the forms require: for instance, whether the deceased had undergone any operation during the final illness, or within a year before death, whether the deceased had been fitted with a pacemaker, and whether or not it had been removed (pacemakers must be removed before cremation to avoid an explosion) (see box, above).

Form C has to be signed by a second doctor, who must be independent of the first, and must also be of not less than five years' standing.

A fee, set annually by the British Medical Association, will be charged for each form completed: the fee was £62 for each form in 2006. Doctors are also entitled to charge travelling expenses when signing forms for cremation. The bill laid before Parliament in June 2006 stopped short of referring death registration to the reformed coroner service. This may change, but in the meantime Forms B and C continue to be required for cremation.

If someone dies in hospital, the forms will be completed by the doctor who treated the patient and another doctor at the same hospital who is not of the same ward. The same fees will be payable.

If the doctor treating the deceased person at all unsure of the cause of death, the coroner must be informed. A post mortem will usually follow, and if death is found to be due to natural causes, there will be no inquest and the coroner will provide a coroner's **Form E** (certificate for cremation, or, where relevant, a coroner's order for burial), for which no fee is charged. A revised Form E was issued in February 2006 to enable local coroners to authorise cremation of British Citizens who had died of natural causes abroad.

This contains the new authorisation, 'I am satisfied that the death occurred outside the British Islands and that the death was by natural causes and no post-mortem examination or inquest is necessary.' Where the coroner is thus involved, **Forms B** and **C** are not required, and no fees are charged. Previously, application for authority to cremate under these circumstances was provided on application to the Home Office, which is no longer involved.

Form F

This has to be signed by the medical referee of the crematorium, stating that he or she is satisfied with the details on **Forms B** and **C**, or the coroner's certificate for the cremation. The medical referee has the authority to prevent cremation taking place and may query details given in the forms supplied. If it is felt necessary, he or she may order a post mortem to take place, or refer the matter to the coroner, if this has not already been done. The relatives of the deceased have no right to prevent this post mortem; if they do not wish it to take place, then they must forego cremation and opt for burial instead. If they do agree to the post mortem, it is quite likely that they will have to pay for it. Cases such as this are extremely unusual, however: the funeral director and crematoria staff will usually notice any anomalies before it reaches the stage of submission to the medical referee. Most crematoria include the fee for the services of the medical referee in the total charge for cremation.

Coroner's order for burial only

In very rare cases where the coroner has a reason for not allowing cremation to take place, he or she will issue a coroner's order for burial only. The coroner may be able to inform the relatives that cremation may be possible at a later date, when the investigations have been completed; the relatives in this case must be prepared to wait for cremation at a later date, or opt for burial.

Documents for cremation

Document	Source	Function	Recipient
registrar's certificate for burial or cremation (green certificate) *or* coroner's certificate for cremation: Form E	registrar	required before funeral can take place	via relative and funeral director to crematorium authorities; Part C returns to registrar
	coroner after post mortem or inquest	replaces Form B/C	
Form A	funeral director or crematorium: to be completed by executor, next of kin or applicant	applies for cremation and confirms arrangements	crematorium
Form B*	doctor or hospital	certifies cause of death	medical referee at crematorium
Form C*†	doctor or hospital, to be completed by second doctor	confirms cause of death	medical referee at crematorium
ashes disposal form (usually reverse of Form A)	funeral director or crematorium: to be completed by executor, next of kin or applicant	confirms arrangements, gives instructions for disposal of ashes	crematorium authorities
Form F	medical referee	confirms information in Forms B & C or E	crematorium authorities
certificate for disposal of cremated remains	crematorium	confirms date and place of cremation	via relatives to burial authorities
certificate of cremation	crematorium	copy of entry in register	executor or next of kin

* Forms B and C are not required if the coroner is involved and issues Form E.

† Form C is not required if a hospital post mortem is conducted by a doctor qualified for more than five years.

If the body of a stillborn child is to be cremated, a special medical certificate has to be completed by a doctor or a registered midwife, who was present at the birth, or who examined the body after birth. No second medical certificate is required, but the medical referee still has to complete **Form F**.

The table on page 83 summarises the function of each form.

Fees

The fees charged by crematoria vary from one district to another, but are generally in the region of £350–£450 (2006), with additional fees sometimes charged for those deceased persons who did not live in the local district. Unlike burial fees, these are not usually doubled, but involved only a relatively small extra charge. Many crematoria have now abandoned this practice and apply the same charges to all, regardless of where they lived. The fee for the medical referee, who has to sign Form F before the cremation can take place, should be included in the crematorium fee. Other fees will include, for example, the doctors' certificates (£62 each) (2006) and the minister who takes the service. All these are normally paid in advance by the funeral director and added to the final funeral account.

The service

Charges for cremation usually include a fee for the use of the crematorium chapel, whether or not it is used for a religious service. The chapel is non-denominational, catering for a range of religions. Some crematoria have a rota of chaplains of various denominations, but usually arrangements for a clergyman to conduct the funeral service are made by the relatives or the funeral director. There is no law requiring a religious service at a funeral, and a small but growing number of people opt for a non-religious funeral service. The British Humanist Association or the National Secular Society will put you in touch with someone in your area who can conduct such services; most funeral directors will be able to refer you to someone, and some are experienced themselves at conducting such services.

Most crematoria have facilities for playing music while the congregation enters and leaves, and this may be chosen by the relatives.

Crematoria work to a strict appointments system, so services must be fairly short, unless a special booking is made for a longer period, which will cost extra. Most crematoria allow 30 minutes between appointments, some allow 45 minutes, and a few only 20 minutes.

 For more details regarding what happens at the service at a crematorium, see pages 119–20. To contact the British Humanist Association, go to www.humanism.org.uk; for the National Secular Society, go to www.secularism.org.uk.

Being present at the cremator

When making arrangements for the cremation, the next of kin or executors can ask to be present when the coffin is placed in the cremator; this is especially relevant for Hindu funerals, where traditionally the next of kin would light the funeral pyre. Usually, two people only are allowed.

Cremated remains

The cremated remains or ashes of the deceased may be scattered in the grounds of the crematorium where the funeral took place, taken away to be scattered elsewhere, kept by the family, or buried in a local churchyard or cemetery after making the necessary arrangements (see the box, below, for scales of fees). The ashes may also be buried in private ground without obtaining permission from any authority, but remember that the law treats the burial of cremated remains in the same way as full burials, and to remove them without a licence from the Home Office is a criminal offence.

Some crematoria are reluctant to arrange the transport of ashes from one locality to another. The funeral director will be able to arrange this, or relatives can make their own arrangements with a national courier for a fee of £20 to £30 within the UK mainland.

If the cremated remains are taken away, the crematorium provides a free certificate (usually required by churchyards or cemeteries)

Fees for disposal of ashes

Crematorium scattering ashes shortly after a funeral	usually no charge
Crematorium storing ashes and scattering later	small fee
Scattering ashes in the grounds of a different crematorium	£25 approx.
Burial of ashes in a churchyard	£81
Burial of ashes in a local cemetery by C of E priest	£33*
Interment of ashes in municipal or private cemeteries	various
Burial of ashes in an existing family grave	various

* Plus the cemetery authority fee

confirming that the cremation has taken place.

Funeral directors will also supply caskets for burial of ashes, or simple urns for storage or scattering. These vary in price from about £15 for a simple urn to several hundred pounds for an elaborate casket. Decisions about or arrangements for the eventual disposal of ashes need not be made at the time of the funeral. However, if there is even the remotest likelihood that the crematorium will *not* be required to scatter the ashes in its grounds, this should be made clear at the outset. It is easy to scatter ashes later, but, obviously, impossible to do anything else with them once they have been scattered. Normally, when signing statutory Form A (see page 81), the applicant must fill in a form on the reverse giving instructions for the ashes.

Since 1999, considerable publicity has been given to the matter of the dignified disposal of human organs removed for medical research during post mortem examinations, especially in relation to babies and small children. Until recently, relatives of such children experienced considerable distress following the revelation of such retention, and additional concern when they discovered that it was not legal for crematoria to cremate these organs separately after the funeral had taken place. In February 2000 the law was changed to allow crematoria to participate in such procedures. Those concerned should consult their local crematorium superintendent, who will be able to give advice.

“ You don't have to decide the arrangements for disposal of ashes at the time of the funeral, but you should tell the crematorium if you don't want to scatter the ashes in its grounds. ”

 A leaflet entitled *What You Should Know About Cremation* provides information about frequently asked questions, and is available from the Cremation Society of Great Britain: www.cremation.org.uk.

Burial arrangements

Despite the fact that fewer than 30 per cent of bereaved relatives choose to have their loved ones buried rather than cremated, those who take this option face increasing difficulties in finding a churchyard or cemetery where the burial can take place. Most of the 1,124 traditional cemeteries in the UK are almost full. However, there are other options available, ranging from eco-friendly grounds to woodland and other green burial sites.

Most **cemeteries** are municipally operated by either district, parish or borough councils, with private companies owning only a small proportion. The Church of England owns many more burial grounds in the form of **churchyards**, but most of these are full or disused, with space available only for the burial of small ashes caskets. Many local authorities, especially those in urban areas, experience considerable difficulty finding ground available for new cemeteries; the growing requirements of land for building new homes, together with the objections of those people living close to the proposed development, greatly restrict the availability of burial space.

However, increasing interest in 'green' funerals has seen the emergence of over 180 woodland burial grounds in the last few years (see page 95). These are not necessarily cheaper than traditional cemeteries, but this practice is set to become one of the major contributory factors in making new burial ground available. Interest in burial on private land is also increasing (see pages 96–7).

“Rising interest in 'green' funerals has led to the emergence of over 180 woodland burial grounds. ”

The arrangements and fees that you need to think about for churchyards are covered on pages 93-4 and if you are interested in finding out about other burial grounds, such a woodland and green burials, see pages 95-6.

Documents for burial

Document	Source	Function	Recipient
registrar's green certificate for burial *or* if inquest is to be held: coroner's order for burial	registrar coroner	required before burial can take place authorises burial	via relative and funeral director to burial authorities; Part C returned to registrar
application for burial in cemetery	from cemetery via funeral director, usually signed by executor, next of kin or other applicant	applies for burial and confirms arrangements	cemetery authorities
grave deeds *or* faculty (see page 130)	cemetery *or* diocese	proves right to grave	burial authorities
copy of entry in burial register (see page 121)	burial authorities	proves burial and locates grave	executor or next of kin

66 The date and time of a funeral cannot be set until the death has been registered. You can then ensure you have all the appropriate papers ready, as shown above. 99

BURIAL IN CEMETERIES

When someone dies and the family decides that the funeral shall involve burial, arrangements for the funeral can be made very quickly. However, the date and time of the funeral should not be confirmed until the death has been registered, and the registrar's certificate for burial or cremation (or the coroner's order for burial, should he or she be thus involved – see page 24) has been obtained. This must be given to the funeral director for onward transmission to the burial authority, or, if a funeral director is not involved, taken directly to the cemetery office. Without this documentation, the funeral cannot proceed.

Most cemeteries are non-denominational, but a few are owned by a particular religious denomination; burial in such places is usually restricted to members of that denomination. Some cemeteries have a section of the ground consecrated by dignitaries of the Church of England, but the opening of new burial grounds is often attended by a service of consecration for the whole of the area. Some cemeteries have ground dedicated to, or reserved for, other specific religious groups, together with a separate section of general ground. In most cemeteries, any type of religious service can be held, or none at all.

Most older cemeteries have a non-denominational chapel in the grounds and can be used for funeral services

when a service in the church is not desired. However, many of these chapels are seldom used: a considerable number have neither lighting nor heating, and some buildings may be damp and dilapidated.

Some cemeteries provide the services of a chaplain for burial services on a rota basis; where this happens there is usually a choice of Roman Catholic, Church of England or Free Church chaplains.

"Most cemeteries are non-denominational, but a few are owned by a particular religious denomination, where burial places are restricted to their members."

Graves in cemeteries

A **lawn grave,** which consists of a headstone with mown grass over and between the grave areas, is now the only option available in most cemeteries; kerbs, surrounds and elaborate memorials are not permitted.

Although people often refer to purchasing a grave plot, in reality this is seldom possible. Grave plots are usually 'leased', with the cemetery authority retaining the rights of ownership. A grave plot may be leased

89

by purchasing the **exclusive right of burial** in that plot for a specific period not exceeding 100 years. Often the period is less, for example, 75 or 50 years.

> ❝ You can apply for interment in a 'common grave' where another person might also be buried. It may be possible to put up a small memorial or plaque. ❞

There is a charge for purchasing this exclusive right of burial, at prices that vary enormously across the country. The fee charged does not usually include the automatic right to bury someone in the plot; for this, a further interment fee will be charged. Thus the cost of burial will usually consist of the fee for purchasing the exclusive right of burial in a particular plot of land, plus the interment fee when the funeral takes place; the cost of digging the grave may be included in this charge, or may be added to it if a gravedigger has to be employed separately. Purchase of the exclusive right of burial also bestows the right to put

a memorial in place, but a further fee will be charged and restrictions are often placed on the type of memorial permitted.

For this type of private grave, a **deed of grant** is issued, sometimes referred to as a certificate of ownership, for which some cemeteries make a charge. The deed should be kept somewhere safe, and the family or executors should know where it is. It may have to be produced in evidence before the grave can be opened for an interment, and the signature of the owner of the deed obtained before the burial can take place. If the owner of the deed has died, the cemetery authority will probably require some alternative disclaimer if the deed has not been re-registered. After the funeral, the deed will be endorsed with details of the burial and returned to the executors.

It is not essential to purchase the exclusive right of burial; indeed, some cemeteries will not permit their clients to do so. Application can be made to the burial authority for interment in what is often called a '**common grave**': in this case, the burial authority reserves the right to bury another person in the same plot, usually with certain restrictions. It may be possible in these situations to put up a small

 One cemetery database is at www.birmingham.gov.uk/cemeteries. The Commonwealth War Graves Commission also offers a search facility: go to www.cwgc.org. On a less serious note, the US website www.findagrave.com will help you to find the grave of your favourite celebrity.

memorial or plaque, but often this is not allowed. In some cemeteries, no interments will take place in such a grave for a set number of years – usually 7 or 14 – after the first burial, except to bury another member of the same family. Indeed, most graves are dug deep enough to allow two or three burials (sometimes more) to take place.

 Check the cemetery's rules on flowers. Some cemeteries do not allow flowers to be planted on graves; many forbid artificial flowers.

Sometimes people are aware that a **family grave** exists in a certain cemetery or churchyard – sometimes the knowledge is limited to a certain town – and they experience considerable difficulty in tracing its exact location. Online UK cemetery databases that can help people with their searches have begun to spring up, with examples in London, Coventry, Hertfordshire, Bristol and York; the number of such databases is likely to increase as popularity grows (see box, opposite).

In the past, cemeteries offered a wide choice of types of grave, with a variety of memorials. **Mausoleums or 'brick' graves** with a bricked (or concrete) floor and brick-built walls could be constructed. In the few

Jargon buster

Common grave When the burial authority has the right to bury another person in the same plot

Deed of grant Confirms the existence of a private grave (see exclusive right of burial)

Exclusive right of burial When a plot is leased for x number of years

Family grave A specific grave where only members of the family can be buried

Lawn grave When grave consists of a headstone with mown grass around it

Mausoleum A large, brick-built construction

Memorials

The cost of maintaining cemeteries has soared, and most modern burial authorities want to make maintenance economic and as easy as possible. Families planning a funeral that involves burial in a local churchyard or cemetery should make enquiries about memorials as soon as possible, as considerable distress can be caused if an elaborate memorial is planned and restrictions are only discovered after the burial has taken place.

The funeral director is frequently involved in these arrangements, and will warn clients of any restrictions he or she knows about; it is important to tell the funeral director of the family's probable intentions regarding a memorial as soon as possible. Some funeral directors provide their own service of memorial masonry; almost all have contact with stonemasons whom they use as subcontractors.

For more information, see pages 129–32.

places where such graves are still available, the formalities and construction can take weeks, and are always very expensive. The funeral will thus take longer to arrange, and higher interment fees may be required in addition to the cost of the grave.

> " There may be no space left in the churchyard, but some churches have separate burial grounds where parishioners have the right of burial. "

Burial fees in cemeteries

Fees for burial in a cemetery vary widely even within the same locality. They are set by the owners, under the terms of the appropriate Acts of Parliament. Fees and regulations are usually displayed at the cemetery. If you telephone or write to the superintendents of local cemeteries, you will be sent lists or brochures, from which you will be able to compare charges and conditions. A cemetery's fee may include the services of an officiant (there may be a rota of Anglican, Catholic and Free Church ministers) and a gravedigger; most will expect the funeral director or person taking responsibility for the funeral to arrange for these services on their own behalf.

In most local authority cemeteries, a higher fee is required for those who are not residents within the local council district; these are usually double the normal fees, but may be treble, or even more. There may be some concessions for former residents and their relatives. Interment fees are less for children than for adults; each cemetery authority fixes its own fees and defines its own age limits.

Most local authority cemeteries have an application form, which must be completed and signed by the next of kin or executor. All fees have to be paid in advance, and the fee and necessary documents sent to the cemetery office by a stipulated date before the funeral. If a funeral director is involved, he or she will deal with this, and add the fees to the funeral account.

A fee will be charged for the placement of a memorial, and a further fee charged by the cemetery if a second inscription is added to the existing memorial following a second burial in the same grave. For a second or subsequent burial to take place, the existing memorial will have to be removed and replaced; the cemetery authority will not normally be involved in this and will charge no fee, but the memorial mason who carries out the work will charge for its removal and replacement, which is normally two separate fees. Funeral directors will generally deal with these charges, again, adding them to the funeral account.

BURIAL IN CHURCHYARDS

Anyone, whether Christian or not, whose permanent address is within the ecclesiastical parish, is in theory entitled to be buried in the parish churchyard, even if he or she dies away from the parish. In practice, there may well be no space left in the churchyard, and this right cannot be transferred to municipal cemeteries. Many old churchyards are closed to further burials, but some churches have arranged to have extended burial grounds separate from the church, where parishioners have the right of burial. Ex-parishioners and non-parishioners with family graves, or those whose close relatives have been buried in the churchyard, have the right of burial there, as does anyone who dies in the parish.

Setting the fee

It is the incumbent (vicar, rector or priest in charge) and the parochial church council (PCC) who decide whether someone who has no right by law or custom to burial in the churchyard may be buried there, and what fee to charge. For a non-parishioner, or someone with no connection with the parish, the charges are likely to be higher than for a parishioner.

Graves in churchyards

Paying a burial fee does not buy the right to choose the location of the grave in the churchyard. The vicar allots the site. Nor does a burial fee entitle you to ownership of the grave or to the exclusive right of burial in that grave.

If you want the exclusive use of a plot in a churchyard, you must apply to the diocesan registrar to reserve a grave space, by a licence called a **faculty**. Although a faculty gives the right to say who can be buried in the plot, the freehold of the ground continues to belong to the Church.

The fee charged by the diocese for a faculty depends on the amount of work that is involved in the petition. It takes about six weeks for a faculty to be granted. As a result, when a person dies, it is too late to get a faculty for him or her, but the relatives could apply for a faculty to reserve the grave for other members of the family.

Anyone who is arranging a burial in a grave reserved by a faculty must produce the faculty or other evidence that proves the deceased's right to the grave.

The incumbent charges a fee for the first and each subsequent interment in a grave reserved by faculty.

 For information on what happens at a burial, see pages 119-20; and then for how to organise a memorial, should you want one, see pages 129-32.

Burial inside a church

Today, any rights an incumbent may have had in the past to consent to a burial inside the church building have become obsolete. Faculties to permit such burials are rarely granted and in urban areas burial in and under a church is prohibited by law.

"Many people ask for charitable donations in place of flowers. The environmental damage caused by cut flower production is also an issue."

Burial fees in churchyards

For people who live within the boundaries of the local parish, certain fees are payable to the local church for funeral services in church followed by burial in the churchyard (see page 93). The fee for a funeral service in church is £87, and for subsequent burial in the churchyard if £160, making a total of £247 (2006).

The fee for burial in a churchyard without having had a service in a church of the parish beforehand is £193 (2006); the same fee is payable if the churchyard burial does not take place immediately following the church service, but takes place on a subsequent occasion. If a graveside

service is held before a churchyard burial, the fee is £87, plus the interment fee of £160; the cost is the same as if the service had been held in the church. No fee is payable for the burial of a stillborn child, or for the funeral or burial of an infant who died within one year of birth.

If, after cremation, the cremated remains or ashes are to be buried in the churchyard, the fee will be £81; there is no difference in the charge for burying ashes loose or in a casket. If the crematorium service has been a simple committal and the funeral service is to be held in the churchyard when the ashes are buried, a further fee of £87 is incurred – the same as for a service held in church. This fee does not apply, however, if the incumbent officiates at the burial of ashes elsewhere and provides a simple service of committal, when a fee of £33 is normally charged. This is the portion of the fee for burial of ashes in a churchyard that is paid directly to the incumbent.

Gravediggers' fees are in addition to the above. If the parish has its own gravedigger, the fee is likely to be less than £150; if the services of a professional gravedigger are required, the fee is likely to be between £150 and £300. These fees vary according to place and circumstances, and may rise annually – sometimes considerably.

Note that these fees increase annually on 1 January.

OTHER BURIAL GROUNDS

Increasingly, burials are occurring in ground other than a churchyard or cemetery.

Eco-friendly burial grounds

Since the introduction of the Charter for the Bereaved (produced in 1996 by the Institute of Burial and Cremation Administration (since renamed the Institute of Cemetery and Crematorium Management, or ICCM) as a response to the government's Citizen's Charter Initiative), a growing number of environmental issues are coming to the fore. Some burial authorities attempt to encourage as natural an environment as possible. This approach helps to maintain the peaceful character of the cemetery and fosters local flowers and wildlife. In burial grounds that adopt green practices, alternatives to memorial stones are encouraged, as much waste material as possible is composted, and less herbicide is used to maintain the grounds. Increasing tree planting can offset carbon dioxide emissions, and timber from lopped trees can be piled decoratively rather than being burnt. All of these moves, however, increase costs for labour and materials, which must be passed on to the clients in the form of increased charges for burials.

An increasing number of people are asking for charitable donations in place of flowers at funerals. Some would feel that a funeral with no flowers is very sad, but probably more would feel that the money spent on providing stacks of elaborate floral tributes, only to be left withering outside the crematorium, could be put to better use. The environmental damage caused by extensive production of cut flowers is also a cause for concern.

Woodland and green burials

In 1994, only one green burial site existed in England; now there are over 180, with many more planned. In Scotland, almost half of local authorities either provide woodland burial facilities, or are planning to do so. These burial grounds concentrate on keeping the environment as natural as possible, and plots are available in meadowland or woodland.

Normally no memorial stone or tablet is permitted, with memorials taking the form of a newly planted tree, sometimes with a name plaque.

 For more about the Citizen's Charter Initiative, see: http://archive.cabinetoffice.gov.uk /servicefirst/1998/response/bk61005.htm. For green funerals, go to www.peace funerals.co.uk, or for the Natural Death Centre go to www.naturaldeath.org.uk.

A number of woodland burial grounds will provide a complete, but simple burial service for about £1,000; if, however, a church service is required beforehand and a traditional hearse and limousines are provided, the cost will rise accordingly.

Where such services are supplied, all materials interred will be degradable and as natural as possible in order to encourage the wild nature of the environment. Rigid-based cardboard coffins are usually supplied or encouraged, and woven willow or bamboo coffins are becoming increasingly popular. Most burial authorities providing these services will be happy to supply advice (as will some local authorities through their websites). Costs and fees vary considerably, and further information should be obtained from the Natural Death Centre (see foot of page 95).

Burials on private land

No law prevents a burial taking place on private land, provided all the normal procedures of registration of the death have been completed, and the coroner, if involved, is satisfied that his or her investigations have also been completed. The Registrar of Births and Deaths will issue the normal green certificate, or the coroner will provide a coroner's certificate for burial; the detachable section (part C) must be completed by the person arranging the burial and returned to the registrar within 14 days of the funeral taking place.

If you are considering this option, a number of serious considerations must be taken into account:

- **You must obtain permission** from the owner of the land where the burial is to take place if it is not your own.
- **You must consult** the local environmental health officer regarding the burial procedure and any possible effect it may have on nearby watercourses, and so on.
- **The presence of a grave** on the property may reduce its value and make any future resale difficult.
- **You must inform** any individual or mortgage company with an interest in the property of your intentions.
- **Notification that a burial** has taken place, together with an accurate map of the location, should be attached to the deeds of the property.
- **If you decide to move** and want to remove the grave to a new location, a licence for exhumation must be obtained from the Home Office; professional assistance may be needed to deal with the exhumation.

Burial on farmland is an option that may be considered by some landowners; this may involve setting up a formal burial ground and require a long-term commitment to the project. Statutory requirements regarding the maintenance of burial records must be observed, and it would be wise to consult local planning authorities. Several such burial grounds have been established, and provide a valuable service to the local community.

Unless a small part of private grounds can be set aside in perpetuity as a private cemetery, which may well be possible on an estate, farm or family house with a large garden, arrangements for burial at home are likely to present difficulties. A reasonable solution to this problem is to arrange for a cremation, and then to scatter or bury the ashes in the garden or field. Technically, an ashes casket buried in private ground is subject to the same laws of exhumation as a coffin; it can, however, legally be moved from one part of the private grounds to another. If ashes caskets are 'buried' *above* ground in, say, a purpose-built rockery or mausoleum, the casket can be moved elsewhere without difficulty.

Burial at sea

Burial at sea may be requested by anyone; it is relatively unusual, fairly complicated and very expensive. All materials disposed of at sea require a licence under the Food and Environmental Protection Act 1985 Part II (FEPA), which is administered by the Department for Environment, Food and Rural Affairs (DEFRA), or the National Assembly for Wales. Application for the necessary licence should be made to the Marine Consents and Environment Unit, DEFRA.

Where granted, the licence takes the form of a letter, and will be issued free of charge. Such licences will include the date and location at which the burial must take place (the Needles off the coast of the Isle of Wight or Newhaven, Sussex, are the only two locations where burials at sea are currently permitted to take place) and other conditions, including specification of the materials and design of the coffin to be used.

Time must be allowed for a reply, and other documentation will be required.

Registration must take place in the district where death occurred, although information may be given at any register office. An application must be made to the coroner on **Form 104** to remove the body from the English mainland; the coroner will grant permission for the body to be removed and buried at sea on **Form 103**. This must be included with the application, together with a copy of the death certificate and a 'Freedom from infection' certificate stating that death was not caused by fever or an

 To contact the Marine Consents and Environment Unit, go to www.mceu.gov.uk and on the site map to to Burial at Sea. The DEFRA website is www.defra.gov.uk and for the National Assembly for Wales, go to www.wales.gov.uk.

infectious disease. Arrangements for a suitable vessel must be made, allowing for the fact that not only must a heavy coffin be carried and lowered into the sea in a respectful way, but also that a number of passengers will want to accompany it on the boat. Local harbourmasters can be a source of relevant information; generally, however, all such arrangements can be made by an experienced funeral director.

No documents are required for scattering or burying ashes at sea.

The coffin

The coffin must be made from solid wood, have many holes drilled in it, and contain suitable heavy weights to ensure that it will sink. Where such burials are preceded by a church service, the coffin should be covered with a pall to cover the holes.

In cases where people are to be buried in a different district to where they died, the funeral director may subcontract to a local colleague.

FUNERALS AWAY FROM HOME IN THE UK

As people move from place to place more often nowadays, they often express a wish to be buried or cremated in a district other than the one in which they died. In such cases, funeral arrangements have to be made in two places: where the death occurred, and where the funeral is to take place. Most funeral directors are accustomed to this, but if the distance involved is too great, the funeral director may subcontract arrangements at the other end to a colleague on the spot.

Bodies are usually conveyed by hearse within the UK, as this is normally the quickest and cheapest form of transport. It is quite possible to send a coffin by rail or air, but this is likely to be more expensive: the coffin must be suitably packaged and covered with hessian, and for air transport, taken to the carrier's cargo department at the airport four hours before despatch. Charges vary according to the distance and route covered, but airlines may charge a special rate for carrying a coffin with a body inside.

The packaged coffin must be accompanied by all the necessary documents for the funeral, and the

 A specialist company dealing with sea burials is Britannia Shipping Company for Burial at Sea Ltd, which can be reached via www.funeralsuk.com/ Alternative_Green_Funerals/sea.htm.

body must normally be embalmed (see page 20) if it is to be conveyed by any form of public transport. It is also normal practice to ensure that a body is embalmed before carrying it any considerable distance by hearse. Most funeral directors will deal with a distant funeral by accompanying the hearse and driver, and hiring bearers at the other end from a local colleague.

> **"Bodies must normally be embalmed before being conveyed on any form of public transport, or if the distance to be travelled is long. "**

FUNERALS AT HOME FOR THOSE WHO DIED ABROAD

If the funeral is to involve burial, all the documents received with the coffin must be taken to the registrar in the district where the funeral will take place, with the relevant papers suitably translated. The funeral director will normally attend to this, or the coroner's office may be able to help. The registrar will issue a 'certificate of no liability to register', which takes the place of the green certificate (see page 54) and is the only document required by burial authorities, whether a church or local authority.

If the funeral is to involve cremation, the local registrar must issue a 'certificate of no liability to register', as in the case of burial, but further paperwork will be required. Normally the funeral director will attend to this. As this will be time-consuming, plans for the funeral must be adjusted accordingly.

- Since 14 February 2006, application for authority to cremate is no longer made to the Home Office but to the coroner (normally the local coroner in whose district the funeral will take place). Once **Form A** is completed, submit it to the coroner together with the documents received from abroad with the coffin. If the coroner is satisfied that death occurred through natural causes and does not order a post mortem or inquest, he or she will issue a revised version of **Form E** for cremation. Documents received from abroad should include an original document (or certified copy of an original document) that gives the specific cause of death. This does not necessarily have to be a death certificate: it may be a consular death certificate or a doctor's or mortuary certificate.

- If originals or certified copies of the relevant documents do not accompany the returned coffin, contact the funeral directors who assisted with the deceased in the country where death occurred.

Alternatively, contact the person who issued the original documents requesting a certified copy. In certain circumstances, the Consular Division of the Foreign and Commonwealth Office (FCO) may be able to help.

- **If documents are in a foreign language,** you must have them officially translated. However, some European countries now use a multi-lingual death certificate, with each relevant section in five languages. In most cases, the coroner will be able to accept documents in most Western European languages. This should be less time-consuming than the previous system of application to the Home Office, but plans for the funeral should take into consideration that there may be possible delays.
- **Take all documents** received from the coroner to the local Register Office to obtain a 'certificate of no liability to register'. This, together with the statutory Form A and the coroner's revised Form E must then be submitted to the crematorium where the funeral is to take place.

Death not due to natural causes

If death appears to have been caused by something other than natural causes, the local coroner must take steps to discover the cause of death. He or she may order a post mortem examination, and if this satisfies the coroner that death did occur from natural causes, the necessary documents will be issued from the Coroner's Office. If the funeral involves burial, the coroner will authorise a 'certificate of no liability to register', which is all that will be required for the funeral to take place. If the funeral involves cremation, the coroner will issue a revised Form E and also authorise the issue of a 'certificate of no liability to register'.

❝ If death is perceived not to have been through natural causes, the coroner must take steps to establish the cause of death. This might involve a post mortem examination. ❞

If the coroner finds that death was not due to natural causes, he or she will order an inquest to be held, the results of which may well be inconclusive due to the embalming or deterioration of the body and the inability to call local witnesses. In such a case, the funeral cannot be held until authority to do so is received from the coroner, and some delay – sometimes considerable – may be involved.

SENDING A BODY ABROAD

When someone who has died in England or Wales is going to be buried or cremated in another country (including Scotland, Northern Ireland and the Channel Islands), permission must first be obtained from the local coroner. **Form 104** gives notice to a coroner of the intention to remove a body from England, which will be supplied by the registrar or funeral director: usually the funeral director deals with this.

If the registrar knows before registration that the body is to be taken out of England, he or she will not issue a certificate for burial or cremation; if, however, such a certificate has already been issued, it must be sent to the coroner together with the 'out of England' form. Four clear working days must normally elapse before the coroner gives permission on **Form 103**. However, in cases of urgency, a personal visit to the coroner's office with all necessary documentation and information concerning the death will, provided the coroner is satisfied, enable the form to be signed and the body removed immediately. If the coroner is investigating the death, he or she will not release the body for removal from England until satisfied that it will not be required for further examination.

There are no legal restrictions on taking cremated remains out of the UK, but other countries may impose their own restrictions. For example:

- **Italy** is the most difficult: the ashes are treated exactly the same as a body, with all the same documents required, together with permission to import from the local prefect of police in the area of intended disposal. A hermetically sealed container is required, the sealing of which must have been witnessed by a representative of the consul.
- **Greece** treats ashes in the same way as an exhumed body, which may not be imported into the country until one year after death.
- **France** requires consular sealing of a hermetically sealed container bearing an engraved plate that gives the name of the deceased, date of death and death certificate number.
- **India** requires a High Commission permit.

Always check specifications with the relevant embassy or consulate.

The Foreign and Commonwealth Office (FCO) website is very helpful for the protocol on what to do when another country is involved in the planning of a funeral. Go to www.fco.gov.uk for more information.

Making the arrangements

Making the arrangements to take a body into another country for burial or cremation is usually an extremely complex matter and should not be contemplated without expert help and advice. Generally, the body must be embalmed and contained in a metal-lined coffin, which must be suitably packaged. All necessary freight documents must be completed, and a death certificate provided for UK customs clearance. Consular requirements of the destination country must be met, and all documents required must be translated and authenticated at the relevant consulate for a fee.

❝A member of the forces who dies while serving may be buried in a military cemetery at public expense if there is one near to where the death occurred.❞

Consular regulations

Consular regulations change frequently, so in every case enquiries should be made at the local consulate of the country concerned. The requirements usually include:

- Consular permission to take the body into the relevant country
- A copy of the death certificate supplied by the registrar, suitably translated
- An official certificate stating the cause of death and a declaration that sanitary regulations for transporting the body will be met
- A certificate of embalming
- A declaration from the funeral director that the coffin contains only the body of the deceased and accompanying clothing and packing
- Details of the route, flight number and date of departure
- A 'freedom from infection' (FFI) certificate
- A certificate of exhumation and a copy of the Home Office licence to exhume, in the case of exhumed bodies
- A passport wherever it is necessary for the body to pass through another country on the way to its destination – this does not apply to air transport
- A consul representative's presence at the sealing of the coffin/crate.

In addition, the consulate will also provide information about formalities that will be required on arrival of the body, and what arrangements must be made beforehand.

 Information on what happens when a body is embalmed is given on page 20. If you have any doubt about making the arrangements for sending a body abroad, it is best to use the services of a funeral director.

DEATH WHILE IN THE ARMED FORCES

The Ministry of Defence (MOD) provides funeral grants to assist the next of kin of military personnel who die in Service with the cost of funeral arrangements.

Grants are available to the next of kin of any full-time member of the armed Forces who died in service before the termination of their period duty. The level of funeral grant awarded depends on the choice of funeral selected by the next of kin, who can choose:

- **A funeral** at public expense for which no grant is to be made, or
- **A private funeral,** in which the MOD arranges and pays for the preparation of the body, the provision of a coffin and its conveyance to the funeral director (including repatriation of the body from overseas). In this case, the lower rate of grant is awarded: £741.90 for a cremation funeral, or £1,216.72 for a funeral involving burial.
- **A private funeral** in which the next of kin meets all subsequent expenses after the MOD has met the cost of conveying the body to the funeral director of the family's choice. In this case, the higher rate of grant is applicable, which is £890.28 for a cremation funeral, or £1,394.77 for a funeral involving burial.

A member of the forces who dies while serving may be buried in a military cemetery by consultation with the appropriate cemetery authorities. This will be arranged at public expense if there is a military cemetery near to where the death occurred.

If someone who was receiving a war disablement pension dies as a result of that disablement or was drawing a constant attendance allowance, the Department for Work and Pensions (DWP) may pay for a simple funeral. The next of kin should contact the Veterans Agency straightaway, before any formal arrangements are made.

 The DWP website is www.dwp.gov.uk and if you need to contact the Veterans Agency, go through www.veteransagency.mod.uk.

Funerals in Scotland

In Scotland, following registration (see pages 60-4), the certificate of registration of death is given to the informant by the registrar. The certificate must then be given to the person in charge of the place of interment or cremation. No part of the certificate is returned to the registrar. Thereafter, it is only burials in Scotland that differ from funerals in England and Wales.

Cremation

The regulations and procedure for cremation are the same as in England and Wales since the Cremation Regulations 1965 brought these into line with those of Scotland.

Burial

In Scotland, a grave is referred to as a lair. As in England, it is possible to purchase the exclusive right of burial in a cemetery or kirkyard plot, either in perpetuity or for a limited period. Cemeteries are administered by the local council. In Scotland, cemetery chapels are rare.

Anyone who dies in Scotland has the right to a Church of Scotland funeral, which will normally be conducted by the Minister of the Parish in which the person lived (or the Minister of the Parish where the deceased was a member of the congregation, if different). There is usually no charge although a donation to church funds is normal.

At burials in urban cemeteries, silk tasselled cords, called courtesy cords, are attached to the coffin. Specific mourners are sent a card beforehand inviting them to hold a cord while the

❝ It is possible to purchase the exclusive right of burial in a cemetery or kirkyard plot. ❞

The information given on these pages only retlates to the differences between England and Wales and Scotland for cremation and burial. For more information, see pages 79-86 for cremations, and pages 87-103 for burials.

coffin bearers take the strain of the lowering. In most areas of the country the cords actually take the weight. Courtesy cords are not used for the burial of cremated remains.

A pad or mattress is often put on top of the coffin as a development of the old custom of putting grass or straw over the coffin to muffle the sound of earth falling on the lid when the grave is filled in.

In Scotland, by tradition, women did not go to the interment in the graveyard after the church service. This practice has been abandoned by and large, although it still survives occasionally, especially in the older generation.

Sending a body abroad

There are no formalities connected with the removal of bodies out of Scotland for either cremation or burial in another country, but you should ensure that the death has been registered in Scotland before moving the body out of Scotland. The procurator fiscal does not have to be informed.

If the body is being taken to England or Wales for burial, the certificate of registration (**Form 14**) or the standard death certificate must be produced for the registrar there. No formal notice has to be given or permission sought when cremated remains are being taken out of the country.

Bringing a body from abroad

There is no need to produce evidence for the registrar in Scotland that the death took place elsewhere. If the body is coming from England or Wales, the person in charge of the place of interment or cremation in Scotland will require the coroner's form permitting the body to be removed.

When a body is brought into Scotland to be cremated, the authority of the Scottish Ministers must be obtained before cremation can be carried out. This means applying to the Scottish Executive Health Department, with any supporting papers, such as a foreign death certificate.

Cremated remains brought into Scotland must be accompanied by a certificate of cremation issued by the crematorium. See also Death abroad on pages 33–5.

> **❝ The death has to be registered in Scotland before the body can be moved out of the country. This is not necessary for cremated remains. ❞**

Useful websites for Scottish funerals include the General Register Office for Scotland (www.gro-scotland.gov.uk) and the Scottish Executive Health Department (www.scotland.gov.uk).

Arranging the funeral service

Either the funeral director or a member of the family should speak to whoever the family wants to officiate at the service, and find out whether he or she is willing to do so and is available at the time planned for holding the ceremony. Mostly, a minister of religion is involved, who should contact the family, visiting them whenever possible, in order to offer consolation and arrange practical details of the service.

Most people feel that a funeral service should be intensely personal, and whoever conducts the service will need to talk with the family so that a fitting tribute to the deceased can be made effectively. The person conducting the funeral service does not have to be a minister of religion; increasingly, funeral services are conducted by a representative of one of the humanist organisations, an experienced funeral director, or a friend of the family.

" More and more services, including the committal, are being held at the church or hall, and only a few family members then go with the coffin to the crematorium. "

CHURCH OF ENGLAND

A Church of England funeral service that is held in church may be conducted by the incumbent or, with his or her permission, by any other clergyman – for instance, the clergyman whose church the deceased normally attended or who is a member or friend of the family.

There is no obligation to hold a service in church; unlike weddings, for which a building or location must be licensed through the registration authority, funeral services may be held in any building, or at the graveside. Increasingly, funeral services involving cremation are held in the crematorium chapel, but if this is not large enough, the service may be held in a village hall or any such suitable building, with only the committal taking place at the crematorium. There is a growing tendency for the whole service, including the committal, to take place at the church or hall; the coffin is then taken away to the crematorium with only one or two direct family members attending as witnesses. Sometimes this procedure is reversed: there is a private committal at the crematorium early in the day, attended by a few family members, and the funeral service proper is subsequently held in a church or hall later in the day.

The local vicar or rector will be accustomed to taking funeral services in crematoria chapels, and may be prevailed upon to conduct such services in other locations. This may be an advantage if a longer form of funeral service is planned, as services in most crematoria are limited to 20–25 minutes, although double time may usually be booked at an extra charge.

The Church of England, in common with most religious denominations, has a form of funeral ceremony, but again, unlike weddings, there is no legal requirement for any form of words to be said. In the UK, unless the

Funeral service fees (2006)

Funeral service in church	£87*
Burial in the churchyard	£160*
Funeral service by the graveside in the churchyard	£87 + £160
Verger's fee	£10–£30**
Organist and use of organ	various
Choir, bell ringers	various
Heating of church	various

* A proportion of these fees is paid to the incumbent as a contribution towards his or her salary, and the remainder to the PCC. The fees are specified by the Archbishop's Council under the Parochial Fees Order, and usually increase annually.

If the church service is followed by burial in a municipal or private cemetery, the church fee of £87 remains the same, but the interment fee (which will probably be considerably more than £160) must be paid to the local authority or owners of the cemetery. Such fees vary considerably, but no interment fee is payable to the church.

** Diocesan guidelines state clearly that the services of a verger should be included in the fee of £87, to be paid out of the proportion allowable to the PCC; in practice, a verger's fee will frequently be charged for funeral services held in church.

dead person had professed another religion, or the relatives have made specific requests, one of the Church of England orders of funeral service will probably be said at the funeral. Most rituals can be adapted according to the preferences of those concerned. For instance, the main part of the service can be held in the church or some other suitable building, with only a few words of committal at the graveside or crematorium, or the whole service can be held where the committal is to take place. A funeral address may be given either in the church or outside, or not at all.

" There is no legal requirement for what words are said, and most rituals can be adapted to the preferences of those involved. "

Many people give a lot of thought to planning the kind of funeral service they would like for their deceased relatives, with readings, poetry and particular pieces of music. Services held in a Church of England church may be more limited due to the liturgical constraints felt by some of the clergy. Most crematoria have facilities for playing recorded music, and those who would prefer music of their own choice in the funeral service or when entering or leaving should ask for this when making

arrangements for the service. If an unusual form of funeral service is planned, special service sheets may be printed; these may be obtained through the funeral director, directly from a local printer, or produced at home by anyone with a computer.

ROMAN CATHOLICS

For a practising Roman Catholic, it is usual to arrange for the priest to say a requiem mass in the local parish church and for him to take the funeral service. A requiem mass in a Roman Catholic church will follow a very precise order. There are no set fees laid down for Roman Catholic priests to charge for funeral services, but it is usual for the deceased's family to make an offering to the church. Cremation is no longer discouraged for Roman Catholics, and crematoria have Roman Catholic priests on their roster, where such rosters are used.

NON-CHRISTIAN FUNERAL ARRANGEMENTS

Denominational burial grounds usually insist on their own form of service. If you are arranging the funeral of someone of a faith different from your own, get in touch as soon as possible with the equivalent of the local parish priest of that denomination to find out what needs to be done.

Buddhists

Buddhism is the main religion in many Far-Eastern countries such as Burma and Nepal, but it is still relatively rare in the UK. After death, Buddhists will have the deceased person wrapped in a plain sheet and prepared for cremation.

Hindus

Hindus do not normally insist on one approved funeral director to handle funerals; there is no central authority for those who adhere to this religion, and rites and customs vary enormously.

Jews

With Orthodox Jews, the body should be buried as soon as possible once the disposal certificate is issued. If a man subscribes to a synagogue burial society, he or his wife or his dependent children will be buried, free, by the society in its cemetery. The funeral and coffin will

 If a secular Jew is appointed as executor, or is responsible for making funeral arrangements, it is essential that enquiries are made into the religious background of the deceased, so that the appropriate rabbi may be contacted.

be very simple, and there will be no flowers. Orthodox Jews are never cremated, and embalming or bequeathing a body for medical purposes is not allowed. Reform non-orthodox Jews are more flexible, and permit cremation. The coffin and funeral will always be simple, but flowers are allowed.

A Jewish burial society may agree to carry out the funeral of a Jew who was not a member of a synagogue and had not been subscribing to any burial society, but his family will be charged for the funeral and the cost will be considerable. There is rarely any difference between the funeral of members of the same synagogue; all are simple.

If a Jew dies when away from home, it is the responsibility of the relatives to bring the body back at their own expense for the synagogue burial society to take over.

Muslims

Muslim communities normally appoint one person to represent them in making funeral arrangements, who will usually deal with one approved funeral director in the locality. The representative will advise on the rules, which are strict and need to be followed as closely as possible.

 For more information on non-Christian funerals see pages 123–6. Christian cult funerals, such as for Mormons and Scientologists, are covered on page 127 as is New Age culture.

Sikhs

After death, men are dressed in a white cotton shroud and turban; young women are dressed in red, and older women in white. The family will almost always want to lay out the body, and will want cremation to take place as soon as possible – in India, it would normally be within 24 hours.

NON-RELIGIOUS SERVICES

There is no necessity to have a religious ceremony, or indeed any kind of ceremony at all, at a funeral. A 2001 report from the British Humanist Association revealed that more non-religious funerals are conducted in England and Wales than in most other European nations put together. However, because some kind of religious ceremony is customary, if you do not want one or the dead person had made it clear that he or she did not want one, it is important that the executor or whoever is in charge of the arrangements makes this known well before the funeral.

If a body is to be buried in a churchyard without a religious ceremony, or with a ceremony held by an officiant of another denomination, you should give the incumbent of the parish 48 hours' notice in writing; in practice, it should be possible to make the necessary arrangements in a telephone conversation. The usual parish regulations and fees still apply, and additional fees for the officiant

Obtaining more information

- The national freethought organisations in London and elsewhere all give help with funerals: they can offer information and advice by telephone or post, send out literature, and sometimes provide officiants for funerals.
- The British Humanist Association (www.humanism.org.uk) has a network of humanist funeral officiants who can be contacted by calling the 24-hour national helpline: 020 7079 3580. Its accredited officiants conducted some 4,800 funerals in 2000, and the number has been rising by an average of 40 per cent each year. The website for the Humanist Society of Scotland is www.humanism-scotland.org.uk.
- The booklet *Funerals without God: A Practical Guide to Non-religious Funerals* can be obtained from the British Humanist Association, and the other organisations can provide literature for which donations would be appreciated.
- Other agencies include the National Secular Society (www.secularism.org.uk), the Rationalist Press Association (www.newhumanist.org.uk) and the South Place Ethical Society (www.ethicalsoc.org.uk).

Burial without a ceremony

If you want no ceremony at all, the usual procedure is for a few members of the family or close friends to attend the committal in silence or with some music being played.

may be involved (see page 94).

If a body is to be buried in a cemetery or cremated at a crematorium without a religious ceremony, tell the funeral director or the authorities at the time the funeral is being arranged. There will normally be no difficulties, provided it is clear that the proceedings will be properly conducted. Where there is not going to be a religious ceremony, whoever is in charge of the funeral arrangements must also make arrangements for the details of the ceremony.

If you want a non-religious ceremony without an officiant, on the lines of a Society of Friends (Quaker) meeting, you must make sure that those present either know already how such a ceremony works or are told at the beginning.

The more usual procedure is to have an officiant who prepares and conducts the ceremony, on the lines of a minister. This may be a member of the family or a close friend, or a representative of an appropriate organisation or a sympathetic religious minister. The only qualification is some experience of handling meetings. Business, professional and labour organisations generally contain such people, as do humanist societies (see box, opposite). Officiants at funerals would expect to be paid a standard fee plus travelling expenses; these are normally about the same as fees set for church ministers.

It will also be possible in some areas for an experienced funeral director to conduct the service. In the circumstances surrounding a funeral arrangement, trusting relationships are often formed very quickly, and some people feel they would rather be helped in this way by the funeral director than someone whom they do not know.

The form of a non-religious ceremony

A non-religious ceremony may take any form, provided it is decent and orderly. The usual procedure is for the officiant to explain the ceremony, after which there may be readings of appropriate prose or poetry, tributes either by the officiant or others present, and the playing of appropriate music. It is common to allow a time of silence when the deceased may be remembered personally, and religious people may offer silent prayers. These ceremonies are not intended to oppose religious funerals, but are alternatives for people who would feel it hypocritical to have a religious service, or who want a respectful celebration of the death that has occurred without a religious emphasis.

Final arrangements

You will need to decide how the press notices and flowers will be handled – make sure everyone involved is happy with your decisions.

PRESS NOTICES

Announcements of deaths are usually made in local papers, and sometimes the national dailies; the cost for an average obituary in a local paper is likely to be about £80, and in a national paper about £150–£300. Newspapers will not normally accept text for obituaries by telephone, unless placed by a funeral director; even then there is a rigorous callback and checking system because of many distressing hoaxes. The papers do not usually ask for evidence that the death has occurred, unless the notice is submitted by someone who is not a relative, executor or funeral director.

National daily newspapers prefer a standard form of announcement, and are likely to restrict the format and words that can be used. Most funeral directors are well aware of the system, and will advise accordingly. The address of the deceased should *not* be inserted into the obituary: too many houses have been burgled while the funeral is taking place. Where there is anxiety about this, the funeral director may be able to supply a member of staff as a 'house sitter' for the duration of the funeral service.

Burglaries

If you are worried that the house may be burgled while the funeral is taking place, the funeral director may be able to provide a member of staff as a 'house sitter'. The funeral director should not incur any additional expenses without the client's authority.

Donations

The majority of funerals currently give people the opportunity of making donations to a nominated charity in

Charitable donations

An increasing number of people ask family and friends to make donations to a nominated charity in memory of the deceased, and regard this as a fitting memorial for the person concerned. Usually, the funeral director will collect and forward donations to the appropriate charity, sending receipts to each donor and providing the charity and family with a list of donations received. The funeral director will not normally charge for this service.

memory of the deceased, as well as, or in place of, flowers (see box, opposite below). This information is usually contained in the obituary, and the funeral director's name and address are given so that information can be given and donations made.

Funeral details

Details of the date, time and place of the funeral can be included in the obituary. Anyone who has not been specifically invited but wishes to attend is expected to arrive independently at the time and place announced in the press. If the family wants to restrict attendance at the funeral, the obituary should state 'private funeral service', or the equivalent; in this case, only those invited by the family should attend. If the family think that a great many people may wish to attend, arrangements may be made for a funeral service in a large church or auditorium followed by cremation or burial which is attended only by the family and close friends; alternatively, a private funeral for the family only may be followed some time later by a memorial service and all who wish to pay their last respects to the deceased may attend. If no details of the time or place are published, it should be assumed that the funeral is to be private.

FLOWERS

The press notice should make clear whether there are to be no flowers, family flowers only, or the option of

Flower cards may be collected and returned if the funeral director is asked to do so.

a memorial donation. A 'no flowers' request should be strictly observed. Flowers are normally sent to the funeral director's premises; most florists are aware of this, and will contact the funeral director to ask what time flowers should be delivered. It is not normal for press notices nowadays to say where flowers should be sent: the funeral director will collect any that are sent to the family home when he or she calls at the house for the funeral service, and will normally supply the family with a list of those who sent flowers when submitting the account.

When a body is buried, flowers are normally left on the grave after it has been filled in. At the crematorium, there will normally be restrictions as to where flowers can be placed, and the length of time they will be displayed: some are on display for only 24 hours after the funeral and others for a week or more. Traditional wreaths are rare nowadays; it is common for the family to request flowers in the form of bouquets or arrangements and, if requested, the funeral director will take them to hospitals or old people's homes after the funeral service has been completed.

Doing it yourself

Many people assume that funerals can only be carried out by professional funeral directors, but it is quite possible for those who want to organise the funeral themselves to do so. Details given in the Charter for the Bereaved (see page 70) supply sufficient information to enable people to undertake their own arrangements.

Generally, when a close relative or friend dies most people prefer someone outside the immediate family circle to undertake responsibility for the funeral arrangements and to attend to all the necessary details. Many want to 'get the funeral over with' as soon as possible, and are reluctant to be involved any more than is necessary in making arrangements for, and participating in, the funeral service. However, human reactions to grief follow a fairly standard pattern (see pages 38–44), and it is an established fact that personal involvement in arrangements for the funeral will assist the grieving process and, for most, hasten a healthy recovery.

Such participation will, for most people, seldom involve more than laying out and dressing the deceased, visiting the deceased in the chapel of rest, providing family bearers to carry the coffin and participating in the funeral service. It is, however, perfectly possible to arrange the whole funeral yourself (see the outline opposite of everything that you need to consider).

Waiting for the funeral

You must decide where the coffined body is to be stored until the funeral takes place. This will usually be a room of the house, which will need to be kept as cool as possible.

❝ If the deceased died in hospital, it may be possible for the body to stay in the mortuary. If not, you need a cool, well-ventilated room. ❞

Ensure that all heating is turned off, and that there is constant ventilation. Some diseases and/or types of drug treatment cause bodily decomposition to begin far more quickly than normal: it may be necessary to arrange for the body to be embalmed (see page 20), especially in summer. Portable air-conditioners may be hired from an

Arranging the funeral

- Collect, wash and dress the body of the deceased person.
- Assuming that the coroner is not involved, collect the doctor's medical certificate of the cause of death and register the death (see pages 45-64).
- Decide on burial or cremation and obtain the necessary papers, complete and submit to the cemetery or crematorium with the appropriate fees (see pages 76-86).
- It is possible to arrange for a burial to take place on your own land, in a garden, field or woodland (see page 95-7).
- Set a date and time for the funeral with the same authorities. If a church service is to be held, consult the church and minister as well. If a minister is to conduct the service, he or she must be asked to do so, again before confirming the time (see pages 87-94).
- Choose a coffin (see below and pages 75-6).
- If the funeral is to involve burial, and the cemetery or churchyard does not provide an inclusive gravedigging service, hire a gravedigger.
- Take the coffin to the funeral in the back of a large estate car, Land Rover or horse and carriage. Hearses and horse-drawn hearses can be hired.
- Plan the service, if there is to be one.

equipment-hire company to help keep the temperature low.

If the deceased died in hospital, it may be possible for the body to remain in the hospital mortuary until the day before the funeral.

Digging a grave

If you are asking a member of the family or a friend to dig the grave, think it through carefully as many cemeteries may be located on heavy clay or stony ground, the digging of which can be extremely difficult. If the grave is to be on private land, consult the environmental health officer (see page 96).

Coffins

Coffins can be purchased from funeral supermarkets, and some funeral directors are willing to supply them. Biodegradable cardboard coffins are now commonplace, and can be obtained from numerous sources starting at about £60 plus delivery: the Natural Death Centre (see box on page 116) can give advice (they can also advise on which crematoria don't insist on a coffin being used at all). The cheaper forms of cardboard coffin have their limitations regarding both strength and appearance, although they have improved greatly in both respects in the last few years. Wickerwork, woven bamboo and willow coffins are also now readily available, and the cost should be comparable with veneered chipboard coffins.

For those with the ability, it is possible to construct a suitable coffin at home. It must be strong enough to cope with the stress imparted by an inert body being carried and lowered by inexpert bearers, and be made of suitable material: some cemeteries will not allow the burial of any metallic coffin or casket. In the case of cremation, the coffin must be made of materials that conform to the specifications laid down by the crematorium; these are usually printed on the application form, and it is normal practice for a signature indicating compliance to be required. A reasonable degree of expertise and experience is required: it is far from funny when a coffin collapses at a funeral, and no one should contemplate beginning a DIY career by making a coffin.

Funeral management schemes

Many funeral directors are eager to see their clients more involved in funeral arrangements, being aware that this will assist with the grieving process. Some offer a service to clients who want to arrange funerals for their relatives themselves, and are prepared to sell them a coffin at a reasonable price, hire out a hearse if so required and provide a management service for a set fee. The service would provide all the necessary documentation, with advice on how and where to make the necessary arrangements.

If, however, a client decides to pay a management fee, buy a coffin, hire a hearse and then pay the funeral director or hospital mortuary to prepare the body for a funeral, rent chapel of rest facilities and so on, the overall cost could possibly approach the cost of a funeral director's basic funeral. However, this is an unlikely scenario: most of those who want to arrange a funeral without a funeral director do so because they want to do as much as possible themselves.

Helpful advice on organising a funeral yourself can be obtained from the Natural Death Centre (www.naturaldeath.org.uk). The centre also publishes the Natural Death Handbook, which gives advice and information on all aspects of arranging and conducting funerals yourself. This can be obtained from the centre at a cost of £14.99 including postage and packing, or £15.50 if paying by credit card.

The funeral

The form of the funeral can be as formal or informal as you like. Sometimes the deceased will have left specific instructions for what he or she would like to happen at their funeral; more often than not, it is up to the relatives to decide. If there is anything you aren't sure about, don't be afraid to ask for help from the minister or leader concerned.

Christian funerals

Traditionally, the cortege (or funeral procession) started at the house where the deceased lived, with the hearse and one or more cars for the mourners travelling by a pre-arranged route to the church or crematorium.

This still frequently happens, but it is as common for the hearse to travel directly to the location of the funeral from the funeral director's premises; the mourners will then be brought to meet it by either their own or the funeral director's vehicles. If the funeral director provides cars for the bereaved relatives, he or she will marshal the cortege and arrange its departure.

Closing of the coffin

It is unlikely nowadays that the funeral director will ask relatives if they would like to witness the closing of the coffin immediately before the funeral, but customs vary in different parts of the UK.

❝ Timing is important, because cemeteries and crematoria work to tight schedules. ❞

Timing is most important, because cemetery and cremation authorities work to a very tight schedule; if the funeral cortege arrives too early or too late, it will probably interfere with the preceding or following funerals. Should it arrive considerably late, especially at the crematorium, it is possible that the funeral service will have to be drastically shortened, or even postponed, to the great distress of the relatives.

The funeral director may walk in front of the hearse as it leaves the deceased's house, and again as it approaches the church or crematorium; this is not only as a mark of respect, but to enable him or her to direct the traffic and keep the funeral cortege together, especially as it leaves a side street to enter a main road. The coffin is traditionally carried into the church or crematorium on the shoulders of four of the funeral director's staff, although in some places a small trolley is used for moving the coffin. At the time of writing, discussions taking place with the Health and Safety Executive have raised serious questions about possible back injury while lifting and carrying coffins on the shoulders, and it is possible that this practice may be curtailed for professional staff.

When members or friends of the family are able to act as bearers, this makes for a closer participation in the funeral, and the funeral director's staff will still be on hand to assist and give directions. Occasionally, at more formal funerals, pall-bearers walk alongside the coffin, apparently fulfilling no purpose. Traditionally, these used to carry the 'pall', a heavy fabric canopy which was held over the coffin. Today, the pall is normally used to cover the coffin in the hearse if it has to travel some considerable distance between towns before the funeral cortege can gather; it is then removed, and the family flowers are placed on the coffin before it moves off.

CREMATION

Traditionally, the funeral service prior to cremation was held in church, with the congregation (or only the chief mourners if the cremation was to be private) travelling to the appropriate crematorium for a brief committal afterwards. Increasingly, funeral services are held entirely in crematorium chapels; the hearse and cars go straight to the crematorium and the bearers carry the coffin into the chapel and place it on the catafalque. Usually, the mourners follow the coffin into the crematorium, led by the minister and funeral director but, increasingly, people prefer to enter the chapel and sit down before the coffin is brought in, or have the coffin brought in before the mourners arrive. This is difficult in crematoria, as access to the crematorium chapel is not possible until mourners at the previous funeral have left. However, it is usually possible for the coffin to be in place before the main mourners arrive.

When the words of committal are spoken, the coffin passes out of sight; it will either sink into a recess or pass through a door, or a curtain will move in front of it. Some people prefer the coffin to remain on the catafalque until the mourners have left the chapel; this option is available if requested. During the funeral service,

" Funeral services are increasingly held entirely in crematorium chapels. People prefer to enter the chapel before the coffin is brought in, or have it carried in first. "

 Most of the information relating to cremations and burials is covered in the preceding chapter - for cremations, see pages 79-86, and for burials, see pages 87-103.

Register of cremations

Each crematorium has to keep a register of cremations. A copy of the entry in the register is obtainable for a small fee.

the funeral director's staff will take flowers from the hearse and place them in the floral display area; when the coffin moves out of sight at committal, the flowers on the coffin will be retrieved and added to the display. Some crematoria will only keep flowers on display for the day following the funeral; others leave them in place for several days, while yet others clear them once a week. When the coffin moves out of sight, it is taken to the committal room to await cremation. Each coffin is loaded individually into a cremator, once the name on the coffin plate has been checked by the crematorium staff. It is illegal to remove the coffin from the crematorium, or (other than the flowers) anything from the coffin, once the committal has been made. When the cremation process is complete, after two or three hours, the ashes are refined separately and placed in carefully labelled containers; each cremator must be cleared before another coffin can be loaded.

Disposal of the ashes

Cremated remains can usually be obtained from the crematorium on the day following the funeral; however, provided notice is given in advance, ashes may be obtained on the same day if the funeral takes place before midday.

There is no law regarding the scattering of cremated remains; ashes can be scattered anywhere, provided that this is done respectfully, and with the consent of the owners or executors of private grounds, such as golf courses, and so on. If desired, the funeral director will arrange to scatter the ashes for clients in a chosen location and will not normally charge for this unless considerable time and travelling expenses are incurred.

The crematorium grounds are usually known as a 'Garden of Remembrance'; such ground is not usually consecrated, and the place

 If a decision is taken to scatter the ashes, and this is to be carried out by the family, it is important to ensure that the mourners stand with the wind blowing from behind them!

 Many churches place quite rigid restrictions on the type of memorials and stone which may be used in churchyards - see pages 129-32.

where ashes are scattered is not normally marked. Some crematoria scatter the ashes around on the surface of the grass or earth; others remove a small portion of turf, pour the ashes on the ground and then replace the turf. Some allow a casket containing the ashes to be buried in the grounds. The family can choose a spot and witness the proceedings if they request to do so; some crematoria charge a fee for this. There is generally no formal ceremony for the scattering of ashes; the burial of a casket is, however, frequently attended by a minister who conducts a brief service of committal.

BURIAL

Where a burial is preceded by a church service, the coffin is taken into the church by the bearers and placed on trestles or a trolley in front of the altar. In Roman Catholic and some other churches, the coffin may be taken into church before the funeral, often the previous evening, and remain there until the funeral service

takes place. Most funeral services in church take about half an hour, although a requiem mass, or the funeral of a well-known member of the church congregation, may take an hour or more. After the service, the bearers will take the coffin from the church, either to the churchyard or, more commonly, to the local cemetery, usually led by the minister and funeral director. If burial is not preceded by a church service, the coffin is carried direct from the hearse to the graveside, where there is normally a short service.

The coffin will be lowered into the grave by the bearers while the words of committal are said; this part of the funeral service is quite brief, and normally lasts about five minutes. In

"Questions have been raised about the safety aspects of professionals lifting and carrying coffins on their shoulders."

Scotland, the coffin is usually lowered by members of the family. Sometimes the mourners throw a token handful of earth into the grave, or each drops a flower on to the coffin; they do not normally (except in Ireland) remain to see the grave filled in – this is done later by the cemetery staff or gravedigger.

When someone is buried in a Church of England churchyard the

Register of burials

A register of burials in the parish is kept by the church; every cemetery has to keep a register of burials and records of who owns a grave plot, and who has already been buried in each grave. A copy of the entry in these registers are obtainable for a small fee.

family is responsible for looking after the grave. The PCC (parochial church council) is responsible for looking after the churchyard generally, and for keeping the paths and unused parts tidy. Some dioceses stipulate that, before a funeral takes place, a contribution must be made towards the upkeep of the churchyard. Municipal and private cemeteries will employ groundsmen to take care of grounds and graves; this upkeep is often difficult and costly, which is why most authorities now stipulate lawn graves only: graves with a simple headstone in line with other headstones, and no kerbs or surrounds to interfere with mechanical mowing. However, where there are gravestones, whether simple or elaborate, the holder of the grave deeds is responsible for their upkeep; this can become very expensive as stones weather and crack, and ground settles over the years. Upkeep of memorial stones is often neglected – another reason why authorities prefer to stipulate lawn graves only.

" The family of the deceased is responsible for looking after the grave in a C of E churchyard. Some insist on a contribution towards the upkeep of the churchyard. "

 For more information about the disposal of ashes, see cremated remains on pages 85-6.

Non-Christian and minority group funerals

In today's multi-ethnic society, and especially in inner-city areas, many funerals do not conform to the traditional Christian approach that has been the main emphasis of this book so far. This section briefly and simply outlines the practices of other faiths, of which there are now large numbers of adherents throughout the UK.

Buddhists

Buddhists of different nationalities have widely varying funeral customs, and nothing can be assumed to be held in common.

Hindus

There are thousands of Hindu deities, which are all held to be manifestations of the same God. The three main deities are Brahma, the Creator; Vishnu, the Preserver; and Shiva, the Destroyer. Hindu belief in reincarnation means that most individuals face death in the hope of achieving a better form in the next round of life. Death is therefore relatively insignificant, although there is likely to be open mourning with much weeping and physical contact by the family and friends. There are normally strong objections to post mortem examinations, which are held to be deeply disrespectful to the dead.

Hindus are always cremated, and never buried. Prior to the cremation, most Hindus bring their dead into a chapel of rest, where the body must be wrapped in a plain sheet and placed on the floor. Most light lamps or candles, and those who come to view will probably burn incense sticks. There are normally no objections to the body being handled by non-Hindus, but this and all burial rites are capable of great variation. The family concerned will be explicit about the rites required by their form of Hinduism. The Asian

> **A post mortem examination is normally refused by a Hindu family as it is held to be deeply disrespectful to the dead.**

Funeral Service arranges Hindu funerals and organises repatriation for those who require a funeral by the Ganges.

Jews

Scattered from their homeland by the Roman army in AD 70, the Jews dispersed across the world and adopted many different practices and interpretations of the Mosaic Law, yet always maintaining their essential unity. Orthodox Jews believe that the Law was literally handed to Moses by God, while Progressive Jews (divided into Reform, Liberal and Conservative groups) believe that the Law, while inspired, was written down and influenced by many different authors. Orthodox Jews are therefore extremely strict on the observation of funeral rites, while Progressive Jews vary in their attitudes.

> **An Orthodox Jew will not be cremated, although it is accepted among some Progressive groups. In some cases, Orthodox rabbis may bury cremated remains in a coffin.**

When a Jew dies, the body is traditionally left for eight minutes while a feather is placed on the mouth and nostrils to give any indications or signs of breathing. Eyes and mouth are then closed by the oldest son, or nearest relative. Many Jews follow the custom of appointing 'wachers': people who stay with the body night and day until the funeral, praying and reciting psalms. The dead are buried as soon as possible. No Orthodox Jew will accept cremation, although it is becoming increasingly favourable among some Progressive groups. Orthodox rabbis will sometimes permit the burial of cremated remains in a full-sized coffin, and say *Kaddish* (the mourner's prayer) for the person concerned.

Jewish funerals are usually arranged by a Jewish funeral agency (such as United Synagogues (www.unitedsynagogue.org.uk)). Otherwise, the local Jewish community will arrange a contract with a Gentile funeral service, under which all Jewish funerals will be carried out according to strict rabbinical control.

The Jewish Bereavement Counselling Service (www.jvisit.org.uk/jbcs/index.htm) offers support to those who have lost loved ones.

To contact the Asian Funeral Service, which is based in Harrow, Middlesex, call 020 8909 3737 or go to www.uk-funerals.co.uk/funeral-directors/middlesex.html.

Muslims

Muslims live according to a strict moral code which has specific prescriptions concerning death and burial. There are numerous Muslim sects, each with its own variation of funeral rites, but in the UK about 90 per cent are Sunni Muslims, and the remaining 10 per cent are almost entirely Shia Muslims.

Muslims are always buried, never cremated. Traditionally, there is no coffin – the body is wrapped in a plain white sheet and buried within 24 hours of death in an unmarked grave, which must be raised between 4 inches and 12 inches from the ground, and must not be walked, sat or stood upon. Most cemeteries in Britain, however, require a coffin for burial or cremation. Many British cemeteries insist on levelling the graves as soon as possible, which has led to some authorities providing special areas for Muslim burials; where there is none, families can suffer great distress. Because of the need for haste in burials, requests for post mortems and organ donation are usually, but not always, refused.

Muslims believe that the soul remains for some time in the body after death, and the body remains conscious of pain. Bodies must therefore be handled with great care and sensitivity, and disposable gloves worn at all times by those handling the body: the body must never be touched directly by a non-Muslim.

> **"** A Muslim funeral service takes a considerable length of time. Relatives and friends carry the coffin at shoulder height, passing it from one to another. **"**

Embalming is not normally practised, but is permissible where the body has to be conveyed over long distances.

The funeral service will take considerable time. There will be ritual washing, at least 30 minutes of prayer at the mosque, possible return to the family home, prayers at the graveside and the filling in of the grave. Relatives and friends will carry the coffin at shoulder height, passing it

Muslims and laying out

Normally, the family will attend to laying out the body, and they will turn the head over the right shoulder to face Mecca, which in the UK is roughly to the southeast. The body will be wrapped in a plain sheet and taken home or to the mosque for ritual washing: men will wash male bodies, and women female. Camphor is normally placed in the armpits and body orifices, and the body will be dressed in clean white cotton clothes or a special white shroud brought back personally from Mecca.

from one to another, and they will want to see the face of the deceased after the final prayer at the graveside. Muslims must be buried facing Mecca, with the head over the right shoulder; hence graves must lie northeast/southwest, with the head at the southwest end. The family will normally perform all rites and ceremonies, together with the imam, the spiritual leader of the local mosque.

Sikhs

Sikhism developed from Hinduism in the fifteenth century and has much in common with it, but with a strong emphasis on militarism. There is a common belief in reincarnation, and the fact of death is normally accepted calmly.

Sikhs are always cremated, never buried; the Sikh family will insist in every instance that their dead are

> ## The Sikh symbols of faith
>
> There are five symbols of faith, which are vitally important to every Sikh.
>
> - The Kesh is the uncut hair, which, for men, is always turbaned.
> - The Kangha is a ritual comb to keep the hair in place; this is never removed.
> - The Kara is a steel bracelet worn on the right wrist (or left if left-handed).
> - The Kirpan is a small symbolic dagger, which may actually vary in size from a brooch to a broadsword – and the Sikh will never be separated from it.
> - The Kaccha are ceremonial undergarments, which are never completely removed, even while bathing.

cremated with all five 'K symbols' present. Considerable diplomacy may be required to satisfy both family and crematorium authorities.

The coffin will normally be taken home and opened for friends and family to pay their last respects and will then be taken either to the *gurdwara*, for the main funeral service, or direct to the crematorium,

" Sometimes a member of the family will take the ashes of the deceased to the Punjab in India for scattering. "

For details about preparing for a Buddhist, Hindu, Jewish, Muslim or Sikh funeral, see pages 123–7. These pages can only ever give you a broad overview as each ethnicity has its own customs.

where the oldest son will, instead of lighting the traditional funeral pyre, press the crematorium button or see the coffin into the cremator. The ashes will be required for scattering in a river or at sea; it is not unusual for one member of the family to take them to India to scatter them in the Punjab.

Stillborn babies, by exception, are usually buried.

Cults

There are now a great variety of Christian cults, or diverging Christian groups, which include the Mormons, Jehovah's Witnesses, Christadelphians, Christian Scientists, Scientologists, the Moonies and the Children of God. For most, while differences in doctrine are held to be immensely important, there is little deviation from orthodox Christian practice as far as funerals are concerned. Funerals may well take longer, however, which may cause difficulties in fitting in with crematorium schedules.

Some groups, such as Bahai and Hare Krishna, are basically Hindu derivants, and may adhere more closely to Hindu funeral rites than any other.

Much New Age culture is basically a westernised form of Hinduism, and those who practise yoga or transcendental meditation may adopt the Hindu philosophies which lie behind them, which will in due course affect the funeral arrangements that will need to be made.

"The many Christian cults with their various differences in doctrine deviate little from orthodox Christian practice when it comes to funerals."

After the funeral

When the funeral service has finished, family and friends often gather for light refreshments at the house of the deceased, at the house of another member of the family, or at a local public house or restaurant.

PAYING FOR THE FUNERAL

The funeral director will submit an account fairly soon after the funeral, and will appreciate payment as soon as possible: he or she has already paid out quite substantial sums for various services to enable the funeral to take place – but will, of course, understand if the account cannot be settled until a grant of probate or letters of administration have been issued, but interest may be charged on the outstanding account after a specified time. All the major banks will release funds from frozen accounts to enable the funeral bill to be paid if provided with a suitable funeral account from the funeral director, together with an original copy of the death certificate. Legally, payment of the funeral bill is the first claim on the estate of the deceased, taking priority over income tax and any other claims.

"Funeral directors understand that sometimes the account cannot be settled until a grant of probate or letters of administration have been issued."

The Account

The funeral director's account should be as detailed as possible, showing separately what has been paid out to doctors, crematoria, ministers and so on, on your behalf, and what is due to his or her company as the fee for professional services rendered. This will enable you to verify that only authorised payments have been made. Any gratuities given to mortuary or cemetery staff by the funeral director are normally considered as part of the inclusive charge; any tips to bearers or others officiating at the funeral would be at the discretion of the client.

All the payments that the funeral director will have made on behalf of the client should be expenses that would inevitably have been incurred; in addition to the necessities, he or she may have been asked to provide flowers, place obituary notices in newspapers, provide catering and service sheets, and so on.

MEMORIALS

Relatives often want to place a memorial tablet or headstone in a churchyard or cemetery where a coffin or ashes casket has been buried. Both churchyards and municipal cemeteries impose restrictions on the size and type of memorial and on the kind of stone that may be used and the type of lettering inscribed on it. Many cemeteries and almost all churchyards currently prohibit kerbs or surrounds to graves, and memorials are often restricted to a headstone or a plinth and vase set at the head of the grave.

Memorials at crematoria

About a week after a cremation has taken place, the crematorium will usually send a brochure to the next of kin explaining what kinds of memorials are available. These are all optional, are not covered by the fees paid for cremation, and are subject to the payment of VAT.

The most popular means of memorial at the crematorium is the 'Book of Remembrance'. Hand-lettered inscriptions in the book usually consist of the name, date of death, and a short epitaph; the charge depends on the length of the entry. The crematorium displays the book, open at the right page, on the anniversary of death or of the funeral: the relatives choose which they prefer. Some crematoria sell a miniature reproduction of the entry as a card, or bound as a booklet, the price of which depends on the quality.

Charges for the erection of memorial plaques or for inscriptions on panels in memorial passages, where available, vary greatly. Some municipal crematoria will allow no memorial other than the entry in the Book of Remembrance.

Some crematoria have a colonnade of niches for ashes called a columbarium; the ashes are either walled in by a plaque or left in an urn in the niche. Most of these are now full, and where there are spaces, charges are high. Some new, private crematoria, however, have recently made extensive provision for these and other similar memorials.

Some new or recently refurbished crematoria provide extensive means of memorial in carefully landscaped grounds. Some have made new provision for the storage or burial of ashes caskets, and one or two have created elaborate water gardens with provision for personal memorials to be set in place.

Other crematoria have memorial trees, or rose bushes; these are usually arranged in beds, where the memorial bush is chosen by the family, the ashes scattered around it, and a small plaque placed nearby. Costs vary, as does the length of time for which the crematorium will provide maintenance before renewing the charge.

All of these will involve special charges, and are usually offered to the bereaved a couple of weeks after the funeral. Do not allow yourself to be pressurised into buying a memorial

129

Charges for the placement of memorials in churchyards

The Archbishops' Council lays down the charges for the placement of memorials in the churchyards of the Church of England. Charges in municipal and private cemeteries vary greatly. Fees in 2006 are as follows:

● Small wooden cross	£17
● Vase (not exceeding 305mm x 203mm x 203mm)	£72
● Tablet for cremated remains (up to 450mm x 300mm)	£72
● Any other memorial, including inscription	£138
● Additional inscription, added later	£33

that is not something you really want. Take time to consider all the options and costs, and discuss the matter thoroughly with all involved. You may decide that you do not want any form of memorial.

Memorials in cemeteries

Municipal and private cemeteries are generally less rigorous in legislating about types of stone and the wording of inscriptions than churchyards, but many authorities, faced with increasing difficulties of maintenance, insist that only 'lawn' graves with a simple headstone will be permitted.

The upkeep of a memorial is the responsibility of the person who arranged for it to be placed in the cemetery: this includes the responsibility for ensuring that the memorial is in a safe condition. Several people have been killed or injured in recent years as the result of collapsing memorial masonry.

Jargon buster

Book of Remembrance Popular means of memorial at a crematorium

Columbarium A niche in a wall at a crematorium where ashes can be walled in or left in an urn

Faculty Special application to the church authorities for reserving a grave

Plaque Panel A small notice with the name and date of death of the deceased, placed near a memorial rosebush or shrub or attached to a panel on a wall in the crematorium grounds

Some older memorials are very unsafe, and their condition causes great concern to cemetery authorities. Often the owners cannot be identified, as families or relatives of those commemorated cannot be traced. In such cases, cemetery authorities have sometimes had to resort to making such memorials safe by laying the masonry flat on the ground over the relevant grave.

Memorials in churchyards

The rules applying to memorials in churchyards are generally more restrictive than in municipal or private cemeteries. Normally each diocese publishes guidelines for memorialisation, and incumbents are increasingly coming under pressure to enforce compliance. Usually, there are limitations as to the size of the memorial, the type of stone and the wording of the inscription. The general rule is that the type of stone used in the memorial must conform to the stone used in the building of the church; thus churches built of Portland stone (or similar) will often restrict memorial stones to either Portland or Purbeck, and will not allow granite or marble; 'flint' churches, on the other hand, will often require granite or similar materials in order to conform to the appearance of the church.

Quite apart from the size limitations imposed by the Archbishops' Council, most churchyards have a maximum permissible size for stone tablets marking the spot where cremated remains (ashes) have been buried; sometimes these are as small as 230 x 230mm, with only a name and date of death allowed as inscriptions. The rules will vary according to traditional practice or the preference of the vicar.

Neither reserving a grave in a churchyard by **faculty**, where this is still possible (see pages 89–92), nor purchasing the exclusive right of burial in a cemetery, automatically provides the right to put up any kind of memorial. For this, approval must be gained from the respective authorities and a fee paid (see panel, opposite).

Anything other than a simple headstone or inscription requires the granting of a faculty, as does any unusual wording. The wording of an inscription must be approved by the incumbent. Many object to colloquialism and informal descriptions, and will generally stipulate that any quotations are either biblical or otherwise religious. The incumbent will advise on how to apply for a faculty, and a fee will be charged for this. It should be noted that a change of incumbent in a parish church may result in a different interpretation of guidelines, and local regulations may be relaxed or tightened accordingly. What was allowed before may not be allowed now.

Cold calling

Bereaved families should beware of 'cold calling' memorial salespeople, who search the local papers for bereavement notices and attempt to make doorstep sales.

Arranging for a memorial

The funeral director or monumental mason will normally apply to the church or cemetery authorities for permission to erect a memorial; a copy of the entry in the burial register or the deeds of the grave may be required before authority is given. After a burial, allow several months for settlement before any memorial is erected or replaced.

Take time when considering and purchasing a memorial. Names of established local firms of monumental masons can be obtained from the National Association of Memorial Masons or the Association of Burial Authorities.

The cost of memorials varies enormously, depending on the type of stone, size, ornamentation, finish and lettering. Before ordering a memorial, ask for a written estimate which states clearly the items and total cost, including any delivery or erection charges and cemetery fees. It is normal for the stonemason to ask for a 50 per cent deposit to be paid by the client on confirmation of the order: this may seem a lot, but if the client changes his or her mind, there is not much the mason can do with the already inscribed stone.

VAT is charged on the provision of a new headstone or on adding a new inscription to an old one; it is not levied on the removal and replacement of existing memorials. The cemetery fee for the erection of a memorial is also exempt from VAT.

Memorials online

With the rapid increase in the number of people who now have access to the internet and email has come the development of an internet memorial business. In addition to websites giving information about grief support services, there are sites that will help you to develop your own web page. While these sites will only last as long as the relevant webmaster is in business, they provide the opportunity for posting a much fuller obituary than is possible in national or local papers, and at considerably less cost. Websites may include photographs, video clips and music (see below).

 Do not, under any circumstances, order a memorial from any source before ascertaining what the burial ground regulations are.

 For adding an obituary to the internet, go to any of these websites: www.in-memoriam-uk.com, www.lovethelife-remembered.com or www.foreveronline.org.

Obtaining probate

Sorting out the affairs of a person who has died can appear to be a bewildering task; certainly, there is usually a lot to do, but taken one step at a time, it should be fairly straightforward. This chapter leads you carefully through each stage.

Applying for probate

The term 'probate' (or 'probate of the will') means a legal document issued to one or more people ('the executors') by the Probate Registry authorising them to deal with an estate. The Probate Registry must grant probate and, until this is done, none of the deceased's property should be sold, given away or disposed of.

If the deceased has not made a will, the next of kin will usually have to apply to the Probate Registry for a document called 'letters of administration'. The flow chart overleaf sets out the essential steps of applying for probate of the will.

When you apply for probate of the will (as executor) or letters of administration (as administrator) you must establish that you are legally entitled to do so. Once granted – known as the **grant of representation** – that document is legal proof that you are entitled to claim the assets of the deceased, not for yourself but in your capacity as personal representative. You must then administer the estate according to the law – either following the will or the rules of intestacy.

DO I NEED TO APPLY FOR PROBATE?

If all the property of the deceased passes automatically to a beneficiary, e.g. where property is held on a joint tenancy, probate may not be necessary. It is, however, normally required if the value of the estate exceeds £5,000, but the Administration of Estates Act 1965 allows some small estates to be administered without obtaining probate. Probate will be required in order to sell or transfer any property held only in the name of the deceased. It would not be needed if the only asset was a house held jointly as beneficial joint tenants.

A house or flat could be advertised for sale soon after the death of the owner, but remember

 The Principal Probate Registry is your first point of contact. Either phone the helpline 0845 302 0900 or go to website hmrc.gov.uk/cto and follow the links to probate. From here you will find links to all relevant websites. The Form PA2 - How to obtain probate, which is available from www.hm-service.gov.uk, is a useful guide to get hold of immediately.

Accounting to HM Revenue & Customs

Where probate is not required, HM Revenue & Customs rules demand an account of all property in the estate. However, normally you deliver only a simplified account if the value of the estate is low-value (meaning no more than £285,000 (2005-06)), or exempt (meaning that the estate is valued at no more than £1 million but there is no tax to pay because of bequests to a surviving spouse or civil partner or charity).

exchanged before probate has been granted.

A lay executor who distributes the assets of an estate without obtaining probate might miss the obligation to submit an account to HM Revenue & Customs for inheritance tax (IHT) purposes, especially where a substantial gift had been made in the seven years prior to the death or for a longer period if there had been a reservation of interest. This failure could result in serious consequences for the executor.

When and why letters of administration are needed

If someone dies intestate – that is, without making a will – the rules of intestacy laid down by Act of Parliament say who can be the administrator and who should benefit from the estate (see pages 171–2). As an administrator you have to apply for letters of administration for exactly

❝ You must be legally entitled to apply for probate of the will or letters of administration. ❞

the same reasons as an executor has to apply for probate. You may run into difficulties if someone else in the family is equally entitled to apply for letters of administration and you cannot agree who should apply. It could also make it hard to decide who will arrange the funeral and who will take charge of the house. Generally speaking, the grant is made to the first applicant but, in the case of a dispute between equally entitled administrators, consult the Registrar of the Probate Registry.

If a will deals with part but not all of the administration (for instance, where the will says who gets what but fails to appoint an executor), the

For more information on how to obtain probate, contact the Probate and Inheritance Tax Helpline on 0845 302 0900 or go to website www.courtservice.gov.uk and click on the 'Forms and Guidance' tab or search for 'probate'.

Applying for probate: the procedure

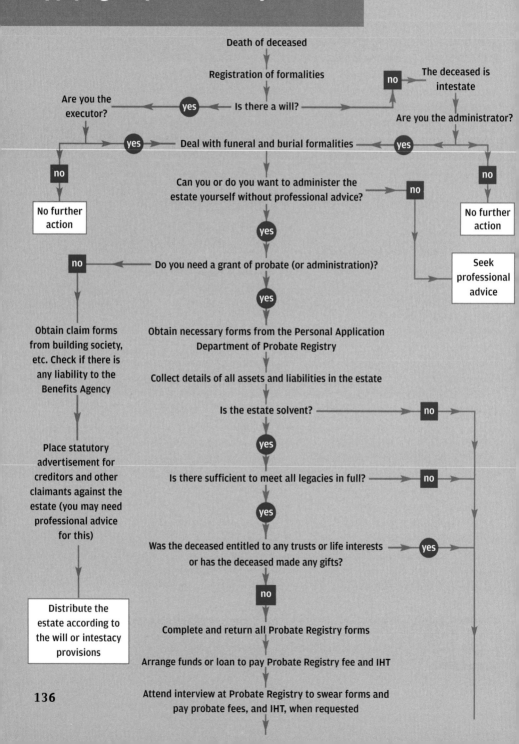

Death of deceased

Registration of formalities

Is there a will? — **no** → The deceased is intestate

yes ← Are you the executor?

Are you the administrator?

yes → Deal with funeral and burial formalities ← **yes**

Are you the executor? **no** → No further action

no → No further action

Can you or do you want to administer the estate yourself without professional advice? — **no** → Seek professional advice

yes

Do you need a grant of probate (or administration)? — **no** → Obtain claim forms from building society, etc. Check if there is any liability to the Benefits Agency

Place statutory advertisement for creditors and other claimants against the estate (you may need professional advice for this)

Distribute the estate according to the will or intestacy provisions

yes

Obtain necessary forms from the Personal Application Department of Probate Registry

Collect details of all assets and liabilities in the estate

Is the estate solvent? — **no** →

yes

Is there sufficient to meet all legacies in full? — **no** →

yes

Was the deceased entitled to any trusts or life interests or has the deceased made any gifts? — **yes** →

no

Complete and return all Probate Registry forms

Arrange funds or loan to pay Probate Registry fee and IHT

Attend interview at Probate Registry to swear forms and pay probate fees, and IHT, when requested

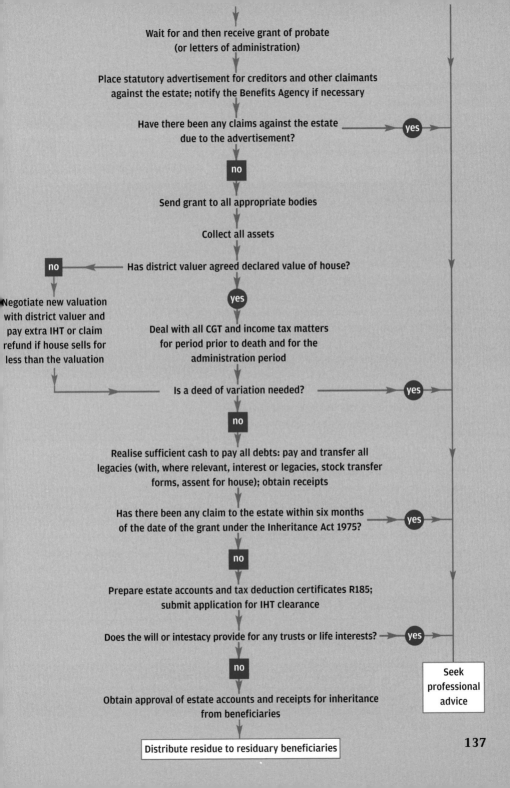

Wait for and then receive grant of probate
(or letters of administration)

Place statutory advertisement for creditors and other claimants
against the estate; notify the Benefits Agency if necessary

Have there been any claims against the estate
due to the advertisement? → **yes** →

no

Send grant to all appropriate bodies

Collect all assets

no ← Has district valuer agreed declared value of house?

Negotiate new valuation
with district valuer and
pay extra IHT or claim
refund if house sells for
less than the valuation

yes

Deal with all CGT and income tax matters
for period prior to death and for the
administration period

Is a deed of variation needed? → **yes** →

no

Realise sufficient cash to pay all debts: pay and transfer all
legacies (with, where relevant, interest or legacies, stock transfer
forms, assent for house); obtain receipts

Has there been any claim to the estate within six months
of the date of the grant under the Inheritance Act 1975? → **yes** →

no

Prepare estate accounts and tax deduction certificates R185;
submit application for IHT clearance

Does the will or intestacy provide for any trusts or life interests? → **yes** →

no

Seek
professional
advice

Obtain approval of estate accounts and receipts for inheritance
from beneficiaries

Distribute residue to residuary beneficiaries

137

Jargon buster

Administration of the estate The task of the executor or administrator

Administrator The name given to a personal representative if not appointed by a valid will. The administrator will usually have to obtain letters of administration to show that he or she is the person with legal authority to deal with the property of the deceased

CGT Capital Gains Tax

Executor The name given to a personal representative if he or she is appointed by a valid will or codicil. The executor will usually have to apply for probate of the will to show that he or she is the person with legal authority to deal with the property of the deceased

Grant of probate The document issued by the probate registry to the executors of a will to authorise them to administer the estate

IHT Inheritance Tax

Letters of administration The document issued by the probate registry to the administer the estate of an intestate

Letters of administration with will annexed The document issued by the probate registry to the administrator when there is a will but the will does not deal with everything, e.g. it fails to appoint an executor

Personal representatives A general term for both administrators and executors

Residue Everything that is left once all debts, liabilities, taxes, costs and legacies have been paid

Solvent Value of the assets exceeeds any debts

person entitled to apply for letters of administration makes the application to the registrar. The applicant, called the **administrator** in this case, is granted 'letters of administration with will annexed'. The applicant can then distribute the estate in accordance with the will or, if the will fails to cover an essential point, in accordance with the rules of intestacy.

> Keep on top of your paperwork at all times; this will help considerably with the procedure. **"**

An important distinction between probate and letters of administration is that administrators have no legal authority to act until the grant of letters of administration is issued to them, whereas executors may act immediately on the death.

 Who can apply for letters of administration? See page 171 for a list setting out in detail the order of those entitled to apply for letters of administration.

Checklist for personal representatives

In cases where the house has to remain empty after the death of its owner it is important for the executor to safeguard the house and its assets. Do not go alone or you may be accused of taking items or money that other beneficiaries believe the deceased had in their possession.

- **Check the insurance** on the house is adequate and valid.
- **Remove any valuables** for safe keeping (don't forget to notify your own insurers if you are looking after the valuables). Make sure the other beneficiaries know what you are doing
- **Advise the police** and see if a neighbour is willing to keep an eye on the house for you.
- **You may wish to keep the services running** but you might find that you have to turn off the water to maintain insurance cover through the winter. Discuss the situation with the insurers

- to make sure you are as fully covered as possible.
- **If there is a car,** it will cease to be covered by the deceased's policy although, as a short-term measure, the insurers may agree to fire and theft cover if it remains in a garage.
- **Arrange with the post office** that all mail will be redirected to one of the executors. An application form can be obtained from any post office. A fee is payable depending on the number of months the service is needed. This forwarding service is useful where a house will be standing empty.

Executors not willing to act

There may be a number of reasons why someone might not want to be an executor: for instance, a relative or friend who had had no contact with the testator for a long period, or someone who simply does not want to be troubled with the chore and responsibilities of the administration.

If you have no wish to take part in the administration, you can renounce probate (obtain a **form of renunciation** from Oyez Straker, see box below). Alternatively, you can take a back seat but remain a potential executor by allowing your fellow executor to apply for probate with 'power reserved' to you. To do this they must serve notice on you (obtain a **power reserved letter** from the probate office).

 To contact Oyez Straker go to website www.oyesformslink.co.uk, and for the Probate Office, go to www.courtservice.gov.uk. In Northern Ireland you will need to contact the Probabe and Matrimonial Office: www.courtsni.gov.uk.

If one of the executors renounces, the substitute (if one is named in the will) automatically comes in, unless he or she also renounces.

It is possible for a person named as executor in the will to appoint an attorney for the purpose of obtaining the grant; the attorney then acts as if he or she had actually been named as the executor in the will. (The appropriate form for this can also be obtained from the Oyez shops.)

A personal representative who has obtained a grant can appoint an attorney to act for him or her in the rest of the administration. Usually the power lasts for one year and relieves a personal representative of the form-signing part of the administration. It can be useful where the executor is abroad. (Since 1985 there have been rules enabling an attorney to act during the incapacity of another, and in some cases this can cover the incapacity of an executor.) The rules are complicated, and, if any question of incapacity through old age or mental illness arises, you should check with the Probate Registry.

DO-IT-YOURSELF

There are examples of people sorting out legal problems themselves and conducting quite complicated cases without legal help. Some 'litigants in person', as they are called, have taken cases to court alone, and many people have bought or sold a house without a solicitor. Whereas a litigant in person and a do-it-yourself house-buyer cannot expect special treatment from the other side, a personal representative will find that special arrangements are in place at the Probate Registry to help him or her to obtain probate without a solicitor. See the chart on pages 136–7 for a step-by-step breakdown of what needs to be done. The Probate Registry form for guidance to apply for probate without a solicitor is PA2. Download it from the Principal Probate Registry website on www.courtservice. gov.uk. Click on the 'Forms and Guidance' tab and then go to 'Probate' in the box 'Work type'.

WHEN TO USE A SOLICITOR

There are, however, some good reasons as to why it might be worth employing a solicitor, which are outlined here:

- **Any number of complexities** can arise in connection with the administration of an estate.
- **Often the personal representatives** are busy people, without the time to cope with the legal side of an administration and would not contemplate administering an estate without employing a solicitor.

❝ If you decide that you want to obtain probate without a solicitor, you will find plenty of guidance at the Probate Registry. ❞

- **The solicitor carries insurance** in case he or she makes a mistake. Another executor making a mistake might be personally liable.
- **A good knowledge of the law** is essential when the deceased owned his or her own business, for instance, or was a partner in a firm, or was involved in an insurance syndicate, or where there is agricultural property, or when family trusts are involved.
- **The same applies** where, on an intestacy or under the will, some of the property is to pass to children who are under the age of 18. Their rights are called minority interests and particular legal problems can arise regarding them.
- **Another situation** that usually requires legal advice is one in which, on an intestacy, some long-forgotten relative is entitled to a share in the estate. The problems involved in tracing relatives who have apparently disappeared generally require careful handling,

as does the situation if they are not found.
- **Homemade wills,** particularly on printed forms, sometimes contain ambiguities or irregularities that can create difficulties, and legal help about the interpretation may be needed to avoid errors. An executor who wrongly interprets a will and fails to distribute to a lawfully entitled beneficiary may well become financially liable for the consequences of his or her mistake.
- **A solicitor** should also be consulted if there is a possibility of anyone seeking a share, or a larger share, of the deceased's estate under the Inheritance (Provision for Family and Dependants) Act 1975.

Solicitors' fees

A solicitor's fees for dealing with an estate are paid out of the deceased's property. They are a legitimate expense, like the funeral expenses and the IHT. The personal

---

Negligence by executors and administrators

If the administration is being conducted by an executor who is also a solicitor, or if you have instructed a solicitor to deal with the administration for you, he or she is liable at law if he or she is negligent. As a solicitor, he or she must hold insurance to cover this possibility.

If you are a lay executor, always take advice when a problem crops up that you do not understand. Otherwise you may be personally liable if things go wrong. If you act on advice from a solicitor (preferably in writing) and the advice is wrong, the solicitor is liable.

If the estate is insolvent –
if the debts exceed the
value of the assets – care is
required. The same applies
where, although the estate
is solvent, there is not
sufficient to pay all the
legacies in full or there is
no residue. If you arrange a
funeral but there is no
money in the estate to
cover it, you will have to
foot the bill.

representatives do not have to pay
them out of their own pockets: along
with any other debts and taxes, legal
costs are usually paid first from the
assets of the estate, after which the
remaining monies are distributed to
the beneficiaries.

Solicitors should charge fees in
accordance with the Solicitors' (Non-
Contentious Business) Remuneration
Order 1994. This sets out the
elements that can affect the final
fee, including the time spent, the
complexity of the estate and its value.
The order also sets out the rights of
clients to information and interest.

Clearly, the charges will be
considerably less for a straightforward
administration than for one in which
complicated matters arise, although
the solicitor may not know about
them at the outset.

If the will states that a bank is to be
the executor, it is worth talking to the
bank at an early stage if you wish to
challenge its fee scales, as banks still
tend to calculate their charges
according to a percentage of the gross
estate. Typical charges would be 5 per
cent of the first £75,000, with 3 per
cent levied on the next £50,000, and
2 per cent on any balance over
£125,000. If the estate is under
£10,000, a minimum charge of £500
may be levied, but there can also be
additional fees.

The application for probate

There is a Personal Application Department in each of the Probate Registries, which has special staff, forms and procedures designed to smooth the path of the inexperienced layman.

However, the help and advice given by the Personal Application Department of a Probate Registry is confined to getting the grant of probate or letters of administration, and the personal representative is generally left to carry out the rest of the administration.

In cases where IHT is payable, the Capital Taxes Office (a branch of HM Revenue & Customs) is geared up to help the layman, but great care is needed to ensure that a mistake or omission does not have financial consequences that fall on the shoulders of the personal representative. You must have a clear understanding of what you are doing and what your obligations are.

> **In cases where IHT is payable you must take great care to ensure no mistakes are made.**

OBTAINING A WILL

If the will is lodged in the bank, the executor has to sign for it or acknowledge its safe receipt in writing if it is sent by post. Where several executors are named in the will, the bank should ask for all their signatures before releasing the will to one of them on the understanding that in due course all the executors will sign an acknowledgement.

Sometimes the will may be held in a solicitor's office safe. There should be no need for the solicitor to keep the will, and he or she should release it to the executors against their signatures if they all sign a receipt for it. If the solicitor is also one of the executors, he or she will expect to be involved in the administration, but if the firm is to deal with the administration of the estate, make sure you are clear about the basis on which the firm will charge (see Solicitors' fees, opposite). If the

 Having trouble finding your local probate registry? Go to website www.lawontheweb.co.uk/basics/probateoffices.htm, which lists each region in England and Wales. For the Capital Taxes Office, go to www.hmrc.gov.uk/cto/.

solicitor who was appointed an executor has left the firm concerned, or has retired, he must be contacted. He may be prepared to renounce as executor, leaving you free to administer the estate without having to use a particular firm of solicitors.

The reading of a will

A formal reading of the will to the family after the funeral is a ritual that now happens mostly (though not entirely) in the world of fiction. It is usual for the executor or administrator to inform the beneficiaries of the contents of the will at an early stage although you should remember that anyone can see a copy once probate has been obtained. There is a slight risk that the will might be found invalid for some reason, or that a later will might be found, or that there is not enough in the estate to pay out all the legacies, so that no legacy can be positively confirmed until after probate is granted and the estate administered. That might be a reason to wait but, otherwise, the beneficiaries might become upset or suspicious if the contents of the will are kept from them.

AN EXECUTOR'S FIRST ACTIONS

Executors have to make sure that all the testator's wishes are carried out as far as is possible. They owe a duty of the utmost faith not only to the deceased but also to the probate court, the creditors of the estate and the beneficiaries. They are under an obligation to realise the maximum benefit from the estate and can be challenged by the beneficiaries or the creditors if they fail to meet their obligations. They must therefore keep all matters of the administration of the estate entirely separate from their own personal affairs and be able to show, later on, by the preparation of estate accounts, that all the assets of the estate could be accounted for.

There are a few things that you should do early on in the proceedings:

- **Once the death** has been registered, obtain copies of the death certificates (see page 52).
- **Establish from the will** that you have full authority to act as an executor, either singly or jointly. If you are a joint executor, decide who is going to do what and get

“A formal reading of the will to the family after the funeral is now something that mainly belongs to the world of fiction. ”

Provisional details of a sample estate

Leave a column at the right-hand side blank so that you can fill in the actual figures alongside the estimates as they become known. Put this provisional list of assets right at the front of a file for easy access.

Assets	£ estimated value	£ actual value
Cash, including money in banks, building societies and National Savings		
Household and personal goods		
Stocks and shares quoted on the Stock Exchange		
Stocks and shares not quoted on the Stock Exchange		
Insurance policies, including bonuses and mortgage protection policies		
Money owed to the person who has died		
Partnership and business interests		
Freehold/leasehold residence of the person who has died		
Other freehold/leasehold residential property		
Other land and buildings		
Any other assets not included above		
SUB-TOTAL		

Liabilities

	£ estimated value	£ actual value
The funeral		
Household bills		
Building Society mortgage		
Probate fees and expenses (approx)		
SUB-TOTAL		

Approximate net value of the estate (assets less liabilities)	

Estimated inheritance tax

Net value of estate	
Less nil-rate band	**285,000**
Estimated IHT @ 40% =	

this down in writing. Even if you divide responsibilities, you will still both have to sign the probate documents and claim forms. You are both legally responsible for the proper administration of the estate.

- **Search the contents** of the deceased's deed box, if it exists. Many important documents might be stored in there, such as a life insurance policy, National Saving Certificates, a building society account book, Premium Bonds and share certificates.
- **Get organised.** It's worth setting up a large file with different sections for each organisation you will be contacting, e.g. bank, insurance company, building society. Take a copy of the will for the file, too. If the original gets damaged in any way, the Probate Registry might raise queries about it.
- **Start preparing a list** of assets, with an estimate as to the value of each (see page 145).

 Provided you keep the necessary receipts and a separate note of the amounts involved, executors are entitled to recover any expenses reasonably incurred in the administration of the estate. On the other hand, you cannot claim payment for time spent.

❝Important documents might be stored in a deed box, so if there is one, make this your first port of call.❞

Valuing of the assets

Now that you have a good idea of what is likely to be involved in administering the estate, write to all the banks, building societies and insurance companies to find out the precise value of each asset.

In these letters you are requesting a **claim form for signature by the executors** and you should include:

- The relevant account or policy number
- A description of the asset
- The fact that you are the executor of the will of the deceased (name in full)
- The name of the co-executor, if there is one, and give his or her address
- A death certificate
- The fact that you will be able to send a copy of the grant of probate once you have received it.

❝ After notification of someone's death, the bank will return cheques marked as 'drawer deceased'. ❞

BANK ACCOUNTS

In addition to obtaining the bank account details, establish if the deceased kept a deposit account at the branch and, if so, the balance at the date of death and the interest accrued to the date of death but not yet added to the account. The deceased might also have kept a deed box at the branch, or otherwise deposited any documents there, and this, too, is worth establishing now.

When a bank is given notice of a customer's death, cheques drawn on that account are returned unpaid with a note 'drawer deceased', and all standing orders or direct debit mandates cease.

- Any cheques drawn by the deceased but not met on presentation because notice of death has been lodged at the bank should be regarded as a debt due from the deceased to the payee.
- If any payments are to be made to the account, the amounts will be held by the bank in a suspense account for the time being.

Cut all plastic cards in half so that they cannot be used fraudulently.

Normally, a bank must not disclose to other people the details of how much is in a customer's account and what securities, deeds or other papers or articles are held, let alone hand them over. The exception is where the information is needed by the executors or administrators after a death so that the IHT accounts can be completed.

> **❝ The only time a bank can disclose other people's account details is when information is needed by an executor or administrator. ❞**

Direct debits

Contact the companies concerned to explain there has been a death and that therefore any direct debits will cease. Let them know that you will settle any outstanding payment when the probate has been granted (if the estate is solvent).

Joint bank accounts

When assets are held in joint names, it may be that the holders intended that, in the event of a death, that person's share would pass to the survivor.

If it is impossible to show who contributed what, or if the items in the account are too numerous or complicated to make it possible to distinguish the sources, the balance might be considered to be held equally by its joint holders.

However, where the joint account holders are husband and wife, it is presumed in the absence of evidence to the contrary that, even if all the money came only from the husband or only from the wife, it is held by them equally. Therefore, half the balance on the date of death would be taken as the value belonging to the spouse who has died. Circumstances may also show that a joint account held by an unmarried couple is owned equally between the joint account holders. It is best to settle any dispute in this area by agreement as the law can be vague on joint ownership disputes.

A joint account held by a couple has the advantage that the survivor can continue to draw on the account even though the other account holder has died. As it can take weeks or even months to get a grant of probate, this allows the survivor to have continued access to ready cash.

The balance in a personal joint account will usually pass automatically to the survivor and so bypasses the will (unless it is a trust account or some other specific agreement was made between the joint account holders). Nevertheless, the share of the deceased is included as an asset of the estate for IHT purposes – unless the survivor is the surviving spouse or civil partner, in which case it is an IHT-exempt transfer.

With any assets held jointly – building society accounts, savings bank accounts and investments, for instance – similar principles apply.

BUILDING SOCIETY ACCOUNT

When you write to a building society, enclose the passbook, if there is one, so that a note of the death can be made on it and to ensure there is no possibility of a fraudulent person making withdrawals on the account.

The amount shown in the book might not necessarily be the current balance of the account because of subsequent payments in or withdrawals, so it is best to ask for confirmation of:

- The capital balance at the date of death
- Interest due but not added to the account at that date
- What interest was credited to the account in the last tax year ending 5 April.

NATIONAL SAVINGS & INVESTMENTS (NS&I)

If there are any NS&I products, such as Savings Certificates and Premium Bonds, to realise:

- Obtain claim form DNS 904 (Death of a holder of NS&I) from the post office.
- Valuations of the various assets will be returned to you together with repayment/transfer forms, depending on how you indicate the assets are to be dealt with.

Where the value of all NS&I Savings accounts or bonds (including

❝A joint account held by a couple has the advantage that the survivor can continue to draw on the account even though the other account holder has died.❞

interest and any Premium Bond prize won since the date of death – see box, below) is £5,000 or less, it may normally be paid out without any grant having been obtained. NS&I will, however, ask if a grant is being obtained and, if so, may refuse to pay without sight of it unless the savings were held jointly or in trust.

Premium Bonds

Premium Bonds do not need to have an official valuation, but you should nevertheless notify NS&I of the bondholder's death as soon as possible (www.nsandi.com). Premium Bonds retain their face value, and no question of interest arises. They cannot be nominated and cannot be transferred to beneficiaries but may be left in the prize draws for 12 calendar months following the death, and then cashed. The money can be reinvested in new bonds in the name of the beneficiary but these will have to wait three months before becoming eligible for inclusion in the prize draw.

Return any prizes received after the bondholder's death to the Bonds and Stock Office for it to determine and confirm that the deceased's estate is eligible and entitled to receive it. Where it happens that a prize warrant has been paid into the deceased's bank account after the date of death but before either the bank or the Bonds and Stock Office has been notified to freeze the account or stop payment, the Bonds and Stock Office will ask for the prize to be returned so that a new warrant can be sent to the executors after probate has been registered.

INSURANCE POLICY

Check through any insurance policy to establish what type it is. If it is a with-profits policy, an additional sum will be paid to you, the executor, by the insurance company. In this instance, when you write to the company, you should ask for confirmation of the amount payable on death in addition to the sum assured.

VALUATION OF PROPERTY

Most people have some idea of the current value of the properties in their locality. It is not essential in the first instance to obtain a professional valuation from a firm of surveyors and valuers.

Whether you have a professional valuation or not, if the estate is large enough to incur IHT, your estimate will be checked sooner or later by an official called the district valuer. The district valuer knows the value of every sale in his or her district so there is no point in trying to understate the value of a house. However, for possible saving on IHT, at this stage you may decide to put down your lowest reasonable estimate of value. The district valuer may query your figure later on if it is too low, but perhaps not if it is on the high side. If there is IHT to pay on the estate, you would be wise to bring in a professional valuer to prepare a valuation in case the district valuer should challenge your valuation.

❝ If the estate is large enough to incur inheritance tax, your estimate of the value of any property will always be checked by an official called the district valuer. ❞

However (particularly in an estate where there is no IHT payable), pushing for a higher estimated value could mean less tax in the long run if there is a possibility that any future sale might be subject to CGT (see pages 158–9). The established value for IHT purposes will be the beneficiary's base cost for CGT purposes, so a low IHT value on death might mean a larger gain on any future sale.

Where a house is not going to be sold, it is possible to agree a value for the house with the district valuer before applying for probate, but this can delay matters.

If the property is jointly owned

There are two different ways in which people may own a house or land jointly: as joint tenants or as tenants in common. Married couples and civil partners usually hold property as joint tenants, and business partners as tenants in common, but this isn't always the case.

- Where a house is owned by **joint tenants**, the share of the first to die passes to the survivor automatically on death. The survivor of joint tenants acquires the other half-share merely by surviving, irrespective of anything the will may say.
- In the case of **tenants in common**, however, the share of the first to die passes according to the will or intestacy. It could pass to the co-owner under the will, but that is not the same thing as the share passing

If you live in Scotland, Scottish law is different in certain places to the law of England and Wales, so turn to pages 173-7 for changes in the law that you need to be aware of.

to him or her automatically, as happens when it is a joint tenancy, and it may go to someone quite different.

- If the property is held as tenants in common, you will have to know the proportions in which it is held (this could be unequal) in order to estimate the value of the share of the deceased at the date of death.
- For joint tenants, it will be half and half (or equal shares if there are more than two joint tenants).

Calculating the share of the house for IHT

Whenever a house is held in the joint names of two people (whether married or not) the value of the deceased person's share has to be declared for IHT purposes.

The vacant possession value at the date of death is the starting point in calculating the value of the deceased's share of the house for IHT. Suppose it is the figure of £200,000. In the case of a joint tenancy or a tenancy in common held in equal shares, that figure must be divided by two to determine the share of the one who has died. This would give a figure of £100,000.

Except where the joint owners are husband and wife or civil partners, HM Revenue & Customs accept that the value of a part share in jointly held property is usually worth less than simply the relevant share of the vacant possession value. This is because on the open market it will generally be hard to find a buyer willing to buy just a part share, especially if the surviving co-owner(s) have the right to stay in the property.

As a starting point, the Revenue allow you to reduce the value of the deceased's share of a property by 10 per cent. In the example above, therefore, the £100,000 share of £200,000 house would be reduced to £90,000 for inheritance tax purposes. However, if the surviving owner has the right to stay in the property, the Revenue should accept

❝ If there is an outstanding mortgage on the property, this must be taken into account when calculating IHT. ❞

 If there is any doubt as to whether the property is in the deceased's name alone or in joint ownership as a joint tenancy or tenancy in common, you must check what the deeds (or title) says.

a 15 per cent reduction. So, in this example, the value of the deceased's share would be £85,000.

When the property is owned jointly by husband and wife

Valuation officers do not allow any such reduction in the value because of what is called 'related property' provisions, which apply under the Inheritance Tax Act. However, if before the death the property was jointly owned by, say, brothers and sisters, or two or more friends, or parent and child, or any two people not married to each other, you should claim the reduction in the valuation.

❝ If the surviving owner has the right to stay in the property, the Revenue should accept a 15 per cent reduction in the value of the deceased's share of the property. ❞

Outstanding mortgage debts

Account must also be taken of any outstanding mortgage debt on jointly owned property. Suppose that it is £20,000; then the deceased's share of this debt would normally be half, that is £10,000. The result would be that the value of the deceased's share of the house (see main text, opposite) less the mortgage debt would be £75,000, assuming 15 per cent discount.

If there is any outstanding mortgage on the property, you need to obtain an exact figure from the mortgage lender showing the position at the date of death. If there is an endowment mortgage, you need to establish its position, too. You must also check when a house is given to the beneficiary. Is the gift free of the mortgage or subject to it?

For the Which? report on inheritance tax, go to the Which? website: www.which.co.uk. Some of the content on the website is only available to subscribers – information for how to subscribe is given on the website. See also the Which? book *Giving and Inheriting* by Jonquil Lowe.

SHARES AND UNIT TRUSTS

For shares and unit trusts, you need to establish what their value was on the day of death.

You can find a rough estimate of what they were worth by looking up the closing prices in the paper. But for IHT purposes, it is necessary to work out their exact price, for which there is an accepted formula for all shares that have been bought and sold on the London Stock Exchange:

- **On any particular day,** there are sales of shares in nearly all the big companies (or plcs), and the prices often vary depending on the prevailing circumstances. At any one time two prices are quoted – the higher is that at which people buy and the lower at which people sell. The closing prices are the two prevailing prices of the share at the time in the afternoon when the stock exchange has closed dealing for the day.
- **To work out the value** that is officially recognised for probate purposes, you need to know the closing prices on the day of the deceased's death. *The Stock Exchange Daily Official List* (see below) gives the closing prices.

- **Take as the figure** a price that is one-quarter up from the lower to the higher figure. If, for example, the two figures in the quotation column are 100p and 104p, then you take 101p as the value; if the two prices are 245p and 255p, then you take 247.5p as the value. The prices quoted in the official list are often prices for every £1 share held; the nominal value of a share may be 20p, 25p, £1, or any one of many other amounts. It bears no relation to the actual value of the holding.

If there is a long list, it is probably better to write to the bank (but you might be charged for the valuation). Alternatively, a stockbroker would be able to provide this information quite easily, either on the telephone in the case of a few quotations, or by letter if there are more. When a stockbroker

Death at a weekend

If the death was at the weekend, prices from the official list for the Friday or for the Monday may be used and you may mix the Friday and Monday prices to the estate's advantage.

 You can access the Stock Exchange Daily Official List (SEDOL) on at www.london stockexchange.co.uk/en-gb/products/informationproducts/historic/hps.htm. Your local reference library may take it, as might a very large branch of a bank, or you can buy it for a relatively small sum from FT Information Services: www.ftid.com.

makes a valuation, his charge is based on a percentage of the value of the shares.

Checking the holdings

Check you have the correct holdings by writing to the registrar of each company concerned. The address of the registrar usually appears on the counterfoil of the dividend warrant. The counterfoil also acts as a certificate of income tax paid, so it is likely that these have been kept in a safe place. If you can't find the counterfoils, it may be because the deceased didn't keep them, or they may be at the bank if the dividends were credited there directly from the company, or they may be at the deceased's accountants. If, after further searching, you still can't find the certificate(s), make a note to get hold of a copy once you have been granted probate. To do this, you will have to contact the relevant company registrar (see box, below) and you will probably have to pay a fee. You also need to remember that some holdings may have a certificate while others may be uncertificated holdings.

Write the standard letter as outlined

Bear in mind that you might later have to account to HM Revenue & Customs for income tax on any income from the securities that you receive while administering the estate.

on page 147 and ask for confirmation of the relevant holdings and whether there is any unclaimed dividend or interest payment held at the offices.

When a company does not want to distribute its dividend but wishes to retain the cash within the company, it will sometimes 'capitalise' the dividend and instead issue additional shares (called a **bonus, or scrip, issue**).

A **rights issue** is when a company offers its shareholders further shares at less than the market price. If, at the date of death, payment for a rights issue is due, contact the registrar to see if he or she will agree to postpone payment until probate is received. If not, the funds would have to be raised elsewhere (from the bank or by a loan from the executors or

Finding a company registrar

There is a book called the *Register of Registrars*, kept in some reference libraries, which gives details of the registrar of each company quoted on the stock exchange. Alternatively, you could telephone the head office of the companies concerned to find the proper address for the registrar.

beneficiaries to the estate), because the payment may secure a valuable asset to the estate. If payment is not made as required, the rights will be lost.

The same point could arise if a deceased person had just acquired shares in a newly privatised company. Sometimes the original subscription will be for only part of the price, and the balance will be payable by the owner of the shares some months later. If the date is missed, the share can be forfeited or lost, so it is important to ensure that the money is available from some source. It is always wise to check the correct procedure with each company's registrar because practice can vary from company to company.

Unit trusts

If you own shares in one company, you do not know how well that company is going to perform and therefore what profits it will earn, which directly affects the value of the shares. Many people consider it sensible to spread the risk by owning shares in a number of larger companies.

Some investment managers have specialised in this, and it is possible to buy units in a pool of investments in which the investment managers specifically aim to spread the risk. With unit trusts, you do not buy and sell specific shares in companies but buy and sell a specific number of units. This 'unit trust' industry is itself very specialised; investment managers now specialise in different funds so that units can be bought in a portfolio consisting, for example, of property companies, of UK companies or of overseas companies.

If the deceased owned such unit trusts, ask the trust manager to confirm the closing prices on the date of death together with the value of the holding.

Ex-dividend

If a price for shares has the letters 'xd' beside it, this means that the price was quoted 'ex-dividend'. This means that if the shares are sold, the seller – not the buyer – will receive the next dividend on these shares. The price the buyer pays is therefore lower than he would otherwise pay, to the extent of the dividend he is foregoing. This is because the company prepares the actual dividend cheques in advance in favour of the owner at that time, so if the shares are sold before the company sends out the cheque on the day the dividend is due, it will still go to the seller. This usually happens about six weeks before the date for payment of dividends.

Because the price does not reflect the full value of the shares, the dividend must be included as another asset in your list. Phone the registrar of the company to find out what the dividend is to be paid on each share. You can then calculate the total. The answer must be included as a separate asset in the HM Revenue & Customs account of the estate.

Private companies

Although older 'Ltd' certificates are still valid, all companies whose shares are quoted on the stock exchange are now registered with the words 'Public Limited Company' or 'plc' at the end of the name. Private companies, whose shares are not quoted on the stock exchange (and which cannot always be freely sold), all have the word 'Limited' or 'Ltd' at the end of their name.

Valuing shares in a private company not quoted on the stock exchange requires expert help. Sometimes the secretary or accountant of the company concerned can state the price at which shares have recently changed hands, and this may be accepted for probate purposes. If not, detailed and possibly difficult negotiations may have to be undertaken and, unless the shares are of comparatively small value, it would be worthwhile to get an accountant to handle the matter. The basis of valuation is different depending upon whether the interest in the company is a minority or a majority shareholding.

❝ Valuing shares is not straightforward - ask the relevant trust manager or company secretary to confirm closing prices on the day of death. ❞

PENSIONS

Quite often a pension scheme provides that a capital sum should become payable on the death of one of its members. For instance, if a member were to die while still an employee – that is, before retirement – the scheme might provide for the return of the contributions that had been made over the years by the member, and from which he or she has derived no benefit, because he or she did not survive to collect the pension.

- If the lump sum that represents this return of contributions were part of the deceased's estate, it would have to be declared for IHT.
- However, in most schemes nowadays it would be paid 'at the trustees' discretion' and not be subject to IHT.
- Such schemes provide that the trustees may select who is to receive the capital sum (but they are bound by the rules of the particular scheme, and some are quite restrictive). However, schemes usually ask their members to fill in an 'expression of wish' form setting out the person or people they would like to receive the lump sum and the trustees will normally take this wish into account.
- Provided the payment is made genuinely at the trustees' discretion (and so the executors have no legal right to enforce the payment), there

is normally no IHT regardless of to whom the payment is made. In very limited cases - for example, where the member was terminally ill and has deliberately acted to increase the death benefit lump sum they leave - IHT could be due but not where the lump sum is left to a surviving spouse, civil partner or dependants.

> **❝ The sum for arrears of pension is a part of the estate and so has to be declared for IHT purposes and included in the probate papers. ❞**

Whatever the circumstances, it is probably best, where the deceased belonged to a pension scheme, to get a letter from the secretary of the pension fund to confirm the exact position regarding what the estate (as distinct from a dependant) is entitled to receive under the scheme. Even if it is only the proportion of the pension due for the last few days of life, obtain a letter to provide written confirmation for the purpose of IHT.

State benefits

If the deceased was receiving state retirement pension and/or other state benefits, such as attendance allowance, winter fuel payment, pension credit or income support, report the death to the Pension Service or Jobcentre Plus using the form which will be given to you by the registrar when you register the death.

The Pension Service or Jobcentre Plus will work out if any arrears of payments are due. These form part of the estate. They have to be declared for IHT and included in the probate paperwork.

INCOME TAX AND CAPITAL GAINS TAX

Income tax is usually based on a person's income received in the tax year that runs from 6 April to 5 April the following year. PAYE works so that a person's tax allowances are spread over the whole year and tax is deducted week by week, or month by month on the assumption that the taxpayer will go on having income throughout the year. If he or she dies during the year, the PAYE assumptions are upset because the taxpayer did not live to receive the income throughout the tax year, and a tax repayment will be due because the full year's allowances can then be set against the income to the date of death. Where the deceased paid tax through self

For further information on benefits and allowances, see pages 199-203. Also, go to the Department of Work and Pensions (www.dwp.gov.uk), HM Revenue & Customs (www.hmrc.gov.uk), Jobcentre Plus (www.jobcentreplus.gov.uk) or the Pension service (www.pensionservice.gov.uk).

assessment rather than PAYE, too little or too much tax may have been paid through their payments on account up to the date of death. Also, if the taxpayer was not liable for tax because his or her income did not exhaust the allowances due, the executor may be entitled to a tax repayment if the deceased received bank interest from which tax had been deducted. Any tax rebates must be included as part of the value of the estate.

You should explain the situation fully to the local inspector of taxes and, if necessary, go to see him or her about any repayment that may be due because too much income tax was levied on the deceased during the tax year in which he or she died. Although tax is claimed only on the amount of income received up to the date of death, tax allowances (such as a single person's or a married person's personal allowance) are granted for the full year, even if the death took place early in the tax year.

If the deceased had an accountant, it might be more convenient to ask him or her to complete the tax return to the date of death.

Depending on the circumstances, you are likely to receive a tax return or a tax claim for completion.

Income received after the date of death

Where income is received after the date of death, you, as the personal representative, will be taxed, either by prior tax deduction or by assessment

 You are given no personal allowances to set against the estate income, but you can set off against the income any interest paid on a loan raised to pay the IHT.

in the normal way. You will not pay the higher tax rate but, on final distribution, you need to provide a certificate (R185) showing what tax has been deducted from the income being passed on to any beneficiaries – see page 190.

Strictly speaking, you should notify HM Revenue & Customs within six months of the relevant year-end and complete a tax return. However, HM Revenue & Customs has recently extended its informal procedure to cover straightforward estates whose income for the administration period does not exceed £10,000. In these cases, the personal representatives can submit a simple computation of the tax liability. In other cases, a self-assessment return will be required.

❝ If the deceased had an accountant, it might be more convenient to ask him or her to complete the tax return to the date of death. ❞

CONTENTS OF PROPERTY AND PERSONAL ASSETS

The next item requiring valuation is the furniture and effects. This includes furniture in the property, household goods of all kinds, jewellery, clothes, the car and all personal possessions. It may not be necessary to prepare a complete list, or to state the respective values of different kinds of articles – but the Capital Taxes Office (who deal with IHT) are becoming more interested in the value of personal belongings and household contents.

Where the person who has died was sharing the house with a husband (or wife) or any other person, it is important to realise that it is only the deceased's household goods, effects, furniture and so on, which need to be included in any valuation for IHT

"If property is held by joint tenants, it will become owned by the surviving owner regardless of the provisions of the will. "

purposes. A husband and wife may have regarded all of the property as being jointly owned by the two of them so that, on the death of either, it becomes wholly owned by the survivor. In such a case, one-half of the value of all the contents should be included. If the deceased owned any particular items outright, the full value of those items will have to be included. (There may be specific items bought by the husband or the wife particularly for him or herself, or acquired by way of inheritance from their own respective families. Such items could quite possibly have been regarded by them as belonging to one or the other, not owned by the two of them jointly.)

You should discuss the matter with the other person concerned to ascertain precisely what was owned by the deceased, what was owned by the other person and what was owned jointly.

It will usually be assumed that, in the case of a husband and wife, the items are owned jointly. If property is held by joint tenants, it will become owned by the surviving owner regardless of the provisions of the will or intestacy, although part of the value will have to be declared for tax purposes. In the case of other people, for example an unmarried couple, it is usually assumed that the person who paid for an item owns it. Obviously, the provisions in a will (or indeed, intestacy) can operate only on the property that is found to be part of the deceased's estate, and no tax is payable on anything owned by someone else.

Valuing a car

The make and age of the car are the principal factors that affect its value;

its condition is another consideration. A study of the prices being asked for second-hand cars by local garages or dealers will give an indication of the value to within about £50. Do not forget to deduct any outstanding loan. If the car is on hire purchase, contact the hire purchase company to obtain its consent to sale (see also box, page 162).

Valuing jewellery

For probate purposes, it is the value for which jewellery could be sold that is needed; insurance value would be the cost of replacement, which is often considerably higher. You will have to pay a valuation fee, for which the jeweller will give you a receipt at the same time as the official valuation certificate. The fee can be included in expenses recovered from the estate due to you as probate representative.

Valuing paintings

When making a calculation of the total value of the effects, it is better to put a separate valuation on items of particular value, such as, say, paintings worth more than about £100. This can be reasonably easy to establish, perhaps because they were recently purchased or had been valued by an expert for insurance (although the insurance value is unlikely to be the same as the probate value). If not, you can obtain a verbal estimate of their value by taking them to a local auction house.

General valuation

More difficult to fix is a value for the great bulk of the household furniture and effects. How do you decide what the tables, chairs, beds, linen, cups and saucers, carpets, TV set, clothes and all the rest of it are actually worth? You have to decide what price

> **❝ It is better to put a separate value on any painting that is worth over, say, £100. This can be reasonably easy to establish. ❞**

they would get if sold to best advantage on the day of death. In practice, this means what they would fetch at an auction. Of course, the second-hand value of the great majority of items is considerably less than the cost when new.

Photographic evidence

From January 2005, HM Revenue & Customs has been paying particular attention to the estimated open-market values given for household and personal goods, so be ready to support your estimates with written and photographic evidence. It even looks at car registration numbers for additional value.

Hire purchase

If there are any items being bought on hire purchase, it is sufficient to take a common-sense attitude by valuing the article as if it had been part of what the deceased owned, along with everything else, and then to treat any outstanding instalments as a debt due from the estate. Where the figures are large, as for example on a car, it might be better to declare the net value as an asset after deducting the outstanding debt, rather than bringing this in as a separate debt.

For IHT, you do not consider the cost of replacement, but the price they would fetch if sold second-hand. The Capital Taxes Office of HM Revenue & Customs does not expect you to provide an expert's valuation, or one that is accurate to within a few pounds, but a valuation that is honest and sensible, and says what the executor really thinks the items are worth. If the estate is liable to IHT expect the revenue to question the accuracy of estimated values.

DEBTS AND LIABILITIES

If anyone owes money to the deceased, include it in the list of property declared for IHT, as these count as assets. They are debts due to the estate. Items such as the dividend on any shares, pensions due to the date of death and any income tax repayment fall within this category.

Debts due from the deceased have to be listed, too. Any money that is owed reduces the estate for the purpose of calculating the total value: the liabilities are deducted from the assets. These debts can consist of almost anything: fuel bills, tax, telephone account, amounts due on credit cards or credit accounts, hire-purchase debts, an overdraft, for example. In addition, the funeral expenses are deducted (but not your expenses for administering the estate).

You will need to contact any companies and individuals that are owed money, explaining that they will be paid soon after probate is granted.

Don't forget the cash

Cash is an asset – don't forget to gather any together and add it to your calculations.

 On page 145 there is a chart to show the provisional details of a sample estate. Continue to refer to it and fill in for your own needs as it gives you prompts for such things as deducting funeral expenses and household bills.

Not enough to meet the debts

In some cases, debts can be a big problem in administering an estate. If you discover that the estate is insolvent, do not continue with the administration and take advice immediately from an insolvency adviser or from a Citizens Advice Bureau (see below), an accountant or a solicitor. It may be necessary to petition the court immediately for a trustee to be appointed to administer the estate – otherwise, you may become personally liable for the debts.

MOVING TOWARDS APPLYING FOR PROBATE

As you receive answers from your letters to the bank, building society, etc., so you can start filling in the right-hand column of the deceased's list of assets and liabilities. Once you've heard from everyone – this could take about a month – you are able to complete the forms that enable you to apply for the grant of probate.

First, though, open an executor's account at your bank, so that you have somewhere specific to transfer money relating to the estate, which is separate from your own bank account.

> **❝ If you discover that the estate is insolvent, do not continue with the administration: stop what you're doing and take immediate advice. ❞**

 To find your nearest Citizens Advice Bureau (CAB) see your local phone book or go to www.adviceguide.org.uk.

Probate application forms

Do not be deterred by the many forms and booklets listed below relating to applying for probate. They are all clearly laid out and designed to make the job as straightforward as possible. If you have any queries, contact the Probate Registry or HM Revenue & Customs (see box at bottom of page).

There are several forms to obtain when applying for probate. From the Probate Registry you need:

- Form PA1: The probate application form
- Form PA1a: Guidance notes
- Booklet PA2: A guide to help a person applying for probate without a solicitor
- Form PA3: A list of probate fees
- Form PA4: A list of probate registries and interview venues.

If the value of the estate is more than £285,000 (2005–06) (including the deceased's share of any jointly owned assets, the value of assets held in trust and any gifts made within the last seven years), from the Capital Taxes Office at HM Revenue & Customs you need:

- IHT 200: The Inland Revenue account
- IHT 210: Notes to help fill in IHT 200
- SP1: Supplementary pages
- IHT (WS): A worksheet to work out the tax
- IHT 213: The notes to help fill in IHT (WS)
- D20 and D21.
- IHT 14: A booklet that sets out the responsibilities of Personal Representations.

If the value of the estate is no more than £285,000 (2005–06) (or no more than £1 million and left largely to your spouse, civil partner and/or charity), from the Capital Taxes Office at HM Revenue & Customs you need:

- IHT 205: Return of estate information

The forms from the Probate Registry can be obtained from www.hmrc.gov.uk/cto or telephone the helpline 0845 302 0900. The HM Revenue & Customs forms can be downloaded from their website: www.hmrc.gov.uk/cto.

- IHT 206: Notes to help fill in IHT 205.
- **Filling in the HM Revenue & Customs forms:** If there is IHT to be paid, you have to fill in these forms and pay the inheritance tax before you make the application for probate. Refer to the notes to help you fill in the relevant forms.
- **Filling in the Probate Registry forms:** Again, there is a booklet and guidance notes to help you fill in these forms. Use them! If you are a co-executor, you will both have to sign the form PA1.

You can either print off forms from the respective websites and complete them in ink, or fill them in interactively.

SENDING OFF THE FORMS AND PAYING INHERITANCE TAX

The back page of the probate application form PA1 sets out a checklist of forms to be sent to the Probate Registry but, where IHT is payable, form IHT 200 must be sent to the Capital Taxes Office rather than the Probate Registry. If there is no IHT to pay, send form IHT 205 to the Probate Registry. The flowchart overleaf shows the sequence of events.

If there is IHT to be paid, this has to be done before the grant of probate can be issued. Inheritance Tax is liable to be paid on the value of an estate over £285,000 (2005–06). It is 40 per cent of the excess. So if, for example, an estate is worth £385,000, the executor would have to pay 40 per cent of £100,000 (£385,000–£285,000), which is £40,000. It is payable to HM Revenue & Customs.

" The Inland Revenue no longer exists. It is now known as HM Revenue & Customs instead. **"**

 You don't have to work out the IHT due yourself. You can submit all your figures to HM Revenue & Customs and they will work out the figure for you – but see page 166 for which forms to send where.

 Some forms and guidance booklets differ in Scotland and it is important to obtain the correct set of forms or guidance booklets for the estate you are dealing with. Full details are obtainable from www.hmrc.gov.uk.

Steps involved in the granting of probate

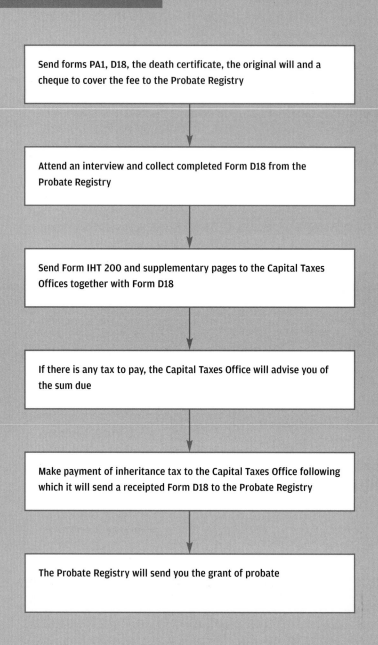

Send forms PA1, D18, the death certificate, the original will and a cheque to cover the fee to the Probate Registry

Attend an interview and collect completed Form D18 from the Probate Registry

Send Form IHT 200 and supplementary pages to the Capital Taxes Offices together with Form D18

If there is any tax to pay, the Capital Taxes Office will advise you of the sum due

Make payment of inheritance tax to the Capital Taxes Office following which it will send a receipted Form D18 to the Probate Registry

The Probate Registry will send you the grant of probate

Raising money to pay IHT

Generally, assets cannot be dealt with before there is a grant of probate. But if the person who died had a bank or building society account, it is possible that the bank or society will release money from the account for the purpose of providing finance for IHT (and probate fees). A cheque will be issued not to you, as executor, but made payable to HM Revenue & Customs for the IHT and to the Paymaster General for the probate fees (you will need form D20).

If the person who died had a Girobank account, you may, subject to satisfactory identification, borrow for the purpose of paying IHT, so that a grant of probate may be obtained. The borrowing is limited to solvent estates and to the amount of the credit balance in the deceased's account.

The Capital Taxes Office provides Form D20 on which to apply to a bank for the IHT to be paid out of the deceased's account. The notes that accompany the forms explain how to fill them in and what to do with them (see the foot of page 164 for obtaining forms).

If this arrangement is not available, you will have to persuade a bank to give you a loan to cover the tax, which can then be repaid once probate has been granted. This can prove difficult if you do not have a friendly bank.

In theory, you can be faced with an odd dilemma. On the one hand, no bank or insurance company that holds money belonging to the estate is willing to hand any of it over to you until a grant of probate is obtained and produced to them; the probate is the only authority that can allow them to part with the money. On the other hand, you cannot obtain a grant of probate until you have actually paid the IHT, or at least most of it. How can you pay the tax without being able to get your hands on the wherewithal to pay it?

Paying the IHT on property by instalment

If there is property to sell that makes up a significant part of the value of the estate, this can reduce the tax payable before getting probate because land and houses are eligible for an instalment option. This means that the IHT due on the value of a house can be paid by ten equal instalments over a period of ten years. Interest is payable but the first payment does not have to be made for six months. As a result, you may not have to raise a loan from the bank, although you will have to pay IHT on the value of the rest of the estate before you get the grant of probate which gives you access to the assets of the estate.

- **If there are funds** in National Savings & Investments accounts (and funds cannot be made available from anywhere else), these can be used to pay the IHT.
- **Also you can use:**
  - NS&I certificates
  - Yearly-plan and Premium Bonds
  - British savings bonds
  - Government stocks on the UK Debt Management Office (DMO) register, administered by Computershare: www-uk.computershare.com
  - Money from save-as-you-earn contracts.
- **A special system** operates between the Personal Application Department of the Probate Registry and NS&I, which enables this to be done. (For obtaining payment from a building society, see page 149.)

IHT payment forms

If you want the Capital Taxes Office to work out the IHT, forms need to be submitted in a different order and to different offices, which are explained on the relevant forms. In addition, if you are submitting Form D20 to a bank or building society, there are other steps that have to be taken:

- Send Forms PA1 and D18 (see page 166) to the Probate Registry together with the original will and an official copy of the death certificate and a cheque for the appropriate amount made payable to HM Paymaster General (the probate fees are £130 and you will also need sealed copies of the probate – ten copies should do – each at £1).
- Following an interview at the Probate Registry (see opposite), Form D18 with Section A is returned, completed by the Probate Registry.
- Complete Form D18 and send it to the Capital Taxes Office together with Form IHT 200 and the supplementary pages. You will then be advised how much IHT is due to be paid. (If you elect to pay the IHT arising on a property, this figure will not be included.)
- To pay, send Form D20 to the relevant bank or building society. Once payment has been made, the Capital Taxes Office will receipt Form D18 (to show IHT has been paid) and send it back to the Probate Registry. Probate will then be granted following an interview at the Probate Registry.

Fees

The probate fees are charges made by the Probate Registry for dealing with the papers and issuing the grant of probate. Form PA4 gives a list of the fees, as a guide. It would be wise, however, to confirm the actual amount payable before you attend the interview at the Probate Registry to swear the papers as this is when you need to pay it. Payment can be made by cheque, banker's draft, postal order or in cash.

AT THE PROBATE REGISTRY

Following the submission of the application for probate, you are given an appointment for an interview at the Probate Registry that is most convenient for you.

All the information that you have supplied will have been translated on to a formal printed legal document, known as the executor's oath. The commissioner will ask you to check the forms to ensure the details are correct – as personal representatives, the executors are responsible for checking that everything is accurately stated (it's worth taking your file of papers with you). Once you are satisfied that everything is in order, sign the oath in the space provided at the end. You will also need to sign the original will and finally swear on oath to affirm the contents of the documents are true. It is a serious offence if you swear or affirm that the contents of the documents are true when you know they are not.

At this point, if it is relevant, you will also be given Form D18 to send with Form IHT 200 to the Capital Taxes Office.

❝ As long as all the forms are filled in correctly, the interview at the Probate Registry should not present any problems. They might even have nothing to ask. ❞

THE GRANT – PROBATE OR LETTERS OF ADMINISTRATION

While there may be an interval of six weeks or more between lodging the probate papers and being asked to come to the Probate Registry to sign and swear them, after that things tend to move quickly. If there is no IHT to be paid, the grant of probate (or letters of administration) will be issued within a few days. If arrangements have to be made to pay the IHT, matters might take a little longer.

Any property that passes by survivorship does not 'devolve to' the personal representatives but goes automatically to the survivor. (This is why it is excluded from the value of the personal estate even though it is not excluded from calculations for IHT, where applicable.)

 The Capital Taxes Office is a department within HM Revenue & Customs – see the website www.hmrc.gov.uk/cto, where you can download all relevant forms, such as D18 and IHT 200 mentioned above.

At the end of the document, the value of the gross and net estate (that is, before and after deduction of debts) is stated, but the amount of tax is not disclosed. The press often publish in the newspapers the value of the estates of famous people who have died. It is seldom a true indication of their wealth because it takes no account of any jointly owned property nor of any trusts to which they are entitled, nor, for that matter, of the IHT to be paid out, which will reduce the estate.

Attached to the grant of probate will be a photocopy of the will, accompanied by a note that briefly explains the procedure for collecting in the estate and advises representatives to obtain legal advice in the event of any dispute or difficulty.

You are now entitled to deal with the deceased's property, pay his or her debts, and then distribute the property in accordance with the will – see pages 187–9.

Remember that the will is a public document in the sense that anybody, including any beneficiary, and even the press, can obtain a copy of it or of the will from Somerset House for a small fee. Copies of the will or the grant can also be obtained at the Probate Registry where they were issued.

❝ When the value of an estate of a famous person is published in the newspapers, it is seldom a true indication of that person's wealth. ❞

Intestacy

This section looks at the thorny issue of intestacy and how a person's estate is distributed when there is no will.

LETTERS OF ADMINISTRATION

When a person has died leaving no will (and recent research shows this could be as many as half the population), the people who administer the estate are called administrators (as opposed to executors, who are named in a will). The procedure adopted by administrators applying for a grant of letters of administration is broadly the same as that adopted by executors applying for a grant of probate, but if the estate is insolvent, a trustee is usually appointed to administer the estate anyway – see page 163.

The nearest relatives, in a fixed order, are entitled to apply for the grant. If the nearest relative does not wish to apply, he or she can renounce his or her right to do so, in which case the next-nearest becomes entitled to be the administrator, and so on, down the line of kinship as set out in the list below.

Order of entitlement

The order of entitlement to apply for letters of administration where the deceased has died intestate (that is, leaving no partially effective will) is:

- The deceased's spouse
- The children of the deceased or their issue*, if a child of the deceased has died before the deceased
- The parents of the deceased
- The brothers and sisters of the whole blood or their issue, if any of the brothers and sisters have died before the deceased
- The brothers or sisters of the half-blood* or their issue (as above)
- The grandparents
- The uncles and aunts of the whole blood or their issue (as above)
- The uncles or aunts of the half-blood or their issue (as above).

* 'Issue' means your children and all subsequent generations arising from them, that is, your grandchildren, your great-grandchildren and so on. Half-blood means sharing only one parent.

If none of these comes forward, the application can be made by the Treasury Solicitor on behalf of the Crown or by a creditor of the deceased.

No distinction is made between legitimate, adopted or illegitimate relationships. They are all treated equally. Normally, an affiliation order or guardianship order from the court would be required to prove an illegitimate child's claim to his or her father's estate, but genetic blood testing can now be used if the deceased father's parents are still alive, and DNA testing can also be used. Step-children have no rights.

An adopted child is deemed to be the legal child of his or her adoptive parents and has exactly the same inheritance right as the adoptive parents' other (natural) children, but adoption removes any rights he or she may have had in law to his or her natural parents' estate. Similarly, the natural parents of an adopted child lose their right to claim against that child under intestacy laws. (However, a natural parent can, of course, still leave property to such a child in his or her will and *vice versa*.)

Distribution on intestacy

When it comes to distributing the estate, administrators must apply the intestacy rules laid down in the Administration of Estates Act 1925.

The division of the net estate where a person has died without leaving a will depends on the value of what is left and what family survives. The net estate is what remains of the estate after paying the debts, the funeral expenses, the expenses of getting letters of administration and administering the estate.

Inheritance tax (IHT) will be payable on the basis of the distribution of the property according to the intestacy rules, that is, no tax is payable on anything that goes to the surviving spouse. Inheritance tax is payable on the balance, once the nil-rate band has been used up.

 Specific laws apply for the distribution of an intestate estate. Anyone considering making a claim under the Inheritance Act (on an intestacy or also where there was a will) should certainly take advice.

Confirmation in Scotland

Inheritance tax (IHT) and its exemptions, including the 'seven-year rule' regarding lifetime gifts and gifts with reservation, apply in Scotland. In other ways, there are considerable differences in law, practice and procedure between the Scots law of wills and succession and the law as it applies in England and Wales.

INTESTACY IN SCOTLAND

The rules of intestacy are set out in the Succession (Scotland) Act 1964 and represent what Parliament then considered to be a reasonable distribution for the average family. Since then, society has changed greatly and the Family Law (Scotland) Act 2006 makes changes to the law to try to take some account of modern lifestyles. For example, cohabitees who are not married to each other (opposite sex relationships) or are in civil partnership with each other (same sex relationships), now have a right to apply to the Sheriff court for a discretionary financial provision from the estate of their deceased partner, if intestate. This right must be exercised within six months of the deceased's death and can be either an award of a capital sum or of a transfer of property. A number of factors have to be taken into account by the court when determining what level of award is appropriate, but a surviving cohabitant will never be better off than if the cohabitant had been married to the deceased. If the deceased left a will, then a surviving cohabitant's right to make a claim in the Sheriff court is defeated.

Under the 1964 Act as amended, the law does not discriminate between children born in or out of marriage or between natural or adopted children. A divorced person or a former civil partner cannot inherit from his or her ex-spouse or ex-civil partner and, where a person with a child later marries or enters into civil partnership, the child cannot inherit from his or her step-parent.

ADMINISTRATORS IN SCOTLAND

All executors have to be officially 'confirmed' by the sheriff court before they can start collecting in the estate. However, confirmation of assets is not always needed. The rules for payments of smaller balances by organisations such as the Department for National Savings are the same in Scotland as in England and Wales. If the only item in the estate is a bank account, it is worth asking the bank for details of its own small estates procedure. Most

bypassing the executor. If confirmation is required for even one item, all assets (cash, personal effects, furniture, car and similar items) have to be entered in an inventory for confirmation. They do not need to be professionally valued, however, and may be valued by the executor. Unless the title to the property contains a survivorship destination (when the share is disclosed for tax purposes only), the deceased's share of joint property must also be confirmed.

will pay up to about £10,000–£15,000 against a formal receipt and indemnity. Confirmation is also unnecessary in the case of joint property where title is subject to a survivorship destination. On death, the deceased's share of the property passes to the other automatically,

ff Assets do not need to be professionally valued and, indeed, this can be done by the executor. **" "**

Declining to be an administrator in Scotland

If an executor-nominate does not wish to act, he or she can decline to be confirmed. A simple signed statement to that effect is all that is needed. You cannot decline but still reserve the right to apply later. If a sole executor-nominate declines, the family may have to apply to the court for another executor to be appointed. In this case, it is quicker and cheaper for the nominated executor to bring someone else in as co-executor and then decline, leaving the co-executor to be confirmed and act alone.

 Useful websites for executors in Scotland include: www.hmrc.gov.uk (HM Revenue & Customs Capital Taxes (Scotland)), www.ros.gov.uk (Registers of Scotland) and www.scotcourts.gov.uk (Sheriff Clerks' Office).

ADMINISTRATOR OF AN INTESTATE ESTATE IN SCOTLAND

For a person who dies intestate, the court appoints an '**executor-dative**'. In this case a member of the family, often the surviving spouse, normally (except for small estates, whose value before deduction of debts does not exceed £30,000) has to petition the court in the place where the deceased was domiciled for appointment as executor-dative. Such petitions are best put in the hands of a solicitor. The court normally handles them within two weeks.

If you are an executor-dative appointed by the court, you are required to supply a guarantee that you will carry out your duties as executor properly before confirmation is issued. This guarantee is called a 'bond of caution' (pronounced 'kayshun') and is usually provided by an insurance company. In recent years the insurance companies have become more difficult about issuing these bonds and the premiums quoted can be quite high. This is an area where almost certainly an executor will require professional help, as the insurers are reluctant to issue bonds to inexperienced executors. Instead of an insurance company, you can, in theory, have an individual as a cautioner but the court would need to be satisfied that, if called upon to do so, the individual is rich enough to pay the sum due. In practice this course is not an option.

Losses caused by the negligence or fraud of an executor are made good by the cautioner in the first instance, with the cautioner then seeking to recover the money from the executor personally.

A bond of caution is not required if you are a surviving spouse and you inherit the whole estate by virtue of your prior rights.

❝ Losses caused by the negligence or fraud of an executor are first made good by a cautioner who then seeks to recover the money from the executor. ❞

 For more information about intestate estates, see pages 171-2.

FIRST FORMALITIES FOR EXECUTORS IN SCOTLAND

Executors, whether nominated in the will or appointed by the court, have limited powers before confirmation. In this period, they should confine themselves to safeguarding and investigating the estate. They should not hand over any items to beneficiaries. Any person who interferes with the deceased's property may be held personally liable for all the deceased's debts, however large. This liability of confirmed executors for debts is limited to the overall value of the estate, providing they acted prudently and within their legal authority before confirmation.

Confirmation forms in Scotland

In addition to the forms outlined on page 164, **Form C1** has to be filled in for confirmation of assets and liabilities. All forms can be downloaded from the HM Revenue & Customs website (www.hmrc.gov.uk). Also, printed copies can be obtained from the Capital Taxes Office or the Commissary Department of the Sheriff Clerks' Office (www.scotcourts. gov.uk). There are no special forms for lay applicants.

Once you, the executor, have all the information regarding the valuation of the assets in the estate and the deceased's debts, you are ready to fill in Form C1 for obtaining confirmation. When there is more than one executor, one of them applies on behalf of all. If there is disagreement among the persons entitled to apply, the sheriff can be asked to make a ruling. An executor appointed by the will who does not wish to act must sign a statement to this effect. This accompanies the application for confirmation.

Post or deliver the form at the Sheriff court for the place where the deceased was domiciled at the time of death. If you are in any doubt, ask your local Sheriff court to advise you. At the same time as you lodge the will, you pay the fee for confirmation. For estates between £5,000 and £50,000, the fee is currently £81; for estates larger than £50,000 the fee is £114. Please note that these fees are liable to be increased without warning.

For an estate with a range of assets, ask for certificates of confirmation for individual items of estate. These cost £3 each if ordered when you apply for confirmation. You can collect the assets simultaneously, using the appropriate certificate of confirmation as evidence of your right to demand and receive them.

 If you think you need to pay inheritance tax (IHT), there are special forms to be filled in. See pages 164–5 for which forms you need and also pages 165–8 for more information on IHT.

Transfer of a property

If the title deed contained a survivorship destination, the executor is not involved in transferring the house of the person who died. The deceased's share of the house is automatically transferred to the surviving co-owner. In other cases, the house must be transferred to a beneficiary under the will or the rules of intestacy and this work should be done by a solicitor. At the same time as the title is transferred, and if money is available, any building society loan can be discharged. Otherwise, arrangements need to be made for the loan to continue under the new owner's name or for a new loan.

After a week or so, if everything is in order, the confirmation is sent to you by post and the will is returned, the court keeping a copy for its records.

PROCEDURE FOR SMALL ESTATES

To reduce the expense of obtaining confirmation, special procedures apply to small estates, which, before deduction of debts, have a gross value of less than £30,000. For a small estate with no will, you do not have to petition the court for appointment of an executor, and the necessary forms are completed for you by the staff at the Sheriff court. Whether or not a will exists, you apply to any convenient Sheriff court by post or in person. You take (or send) to the court:

- A list of all assets and their values
- A list of debts (including the funeral account)
- The deceased's full name and address, date of birth and date and place of death
- The will, if there is one.

The sheriff clerk then prepares the appropriate form for you to sign then and there or to return in a few days' time. The fee for confirmation is payable on signing the form. No fee is charged if the estate is below £5,000. Above that figure, the fee is currently £81. A few days after you have signed the form, confirmation is sent to you by post or to the executor-dative appointed by the court. The will is returned, with the court keeping a copy for its records.

❝ Confirmation is always sent to the executor through the post together with the will. A copy is kept with the court for its records. ❞

Probate in Northern Ireland

The law on wills and probate in Northern Ireland is similar to that in England and Wales. In fact, the law relating to wills is almost identical, following legislation passed on 1 January 1995. This legislation generally applies to wills made both before and after this date, regardless of when the testator died. As for probate, the laws also vary between England and Wales and Northern Ireland and these differences are covered here.

The Administration of Estates Act 1925 does not apply in Northern Ireland. The equivalent legislation is the Administration of Estates Act (Northern Ireland) 1955. Likewise, the Trustee Act 2000 does not apply in Northern Ireland. However, the Trustee Act (NI) 2001, which is very similar to the Trustee Act 2000, came into force on 29 July 2002.

One major difference between England and Wales and Northern Ireland has been created by the 1995 legislation. In Northern Ireland, provided the will is actually signed after 1 January 1995, a married minor or minors who have been married can now make a valid will. However, it is not possible for a married minor in England and Wales to make a valid will.

After someone dies and probate has been obtained, anyone can apply to see it or obtain a copy of it at the Probate Office, Royal Courts of Justice (see below). If it is more than five years since the grant was obtained, application should be made to the Public Record Office of Northern Ireland (see also below).

❝ After probate has been attained, anyone can apply to see it. ❞

 The website for the Royal Courts of Justice is www.courtsni.gov.uk, or to get in touch with the Public Record Office of Northern Ireland, go to www.proni.gov.uk.

DIFFERENCES BETWEEN ENGLAND AND WALES AND NORTHERN IRELAND

Use the basic information already given for England and Wales on pages 133–70, but take into account the special conditions in Northern Ireland relating to the issues discussed below.

Death of husband and wife

In Northern Ireland, the common-law presumption of simultaneous deaths in cases where it is not certain who died first still applies.

Solicitors' fees

There is no recommended scale of fees for solicitors. However, the profession in Northern Ireland tends to follow these guidelines:

- On the first £10,000 of the gross value of the estate: 2½ per cent
- On the next £20,000: 2 per cent
- On the next £220,000: 1½ per cent.

Where the gross value of the estate includes the principal private dwellinghouse, the house's value is normally reduced by 50 per cent for the purpose of calculating fees. In addition to these 'standard' fees, the time spent by various members of staff in the solicitor's office is also costed and charged.

Executor not wishing to act

Only if the executor resides outside Northern Ireland or is incapable of managing his or her own affairs and a controller has been appointed by the Office of Care and Protection, can a person named as an executor in a will appoint an attorney. So, when you make your will, make sure that your nominated executors are willing to serve.

Advertising for creditors

The special procedure for formally advertising for creditors in Northern Ireland requires both an advertisement in the *Belfast Gazette* and an advertisement twice in each of any two daily newspapers printed and published in Northern Ireland. If the assets include land, the advertisements should be in the *Belfast Gazette* and in any two newspapers circulating in the district where the land is situated.

❝ If assets include land, advertising for creditors needs to be done in a different way to assets not including land, as explained above. ❞

Applying for probate forms

Personal applications should be made to the Probate and Matrimonial Office, Royal Courts of Justice in Belfast, or the District Probate Registry in Londonderry. If the deceased had a fixed place of abode within the counties of Fermanagh, Londonderry or Tyrone, application may be made to either address. If the deceased resided elsewhere in Northern Ireland, the application must be made to the Belfast office (for contact details, see below). The fees in all applications are based on the net value of the estate (see box, below).

There is currently no additional fee to be paid for a personal application. Personal applications must be made in person – that is, not by post. The fees increase from time to time with little prior warning, so it is best to check with the appropriate Probate Office before writing the cheque.

Inheritance tax payments

The cheque for inheritance tax (IHT) due should be made out to 'HM Revenue & Customs' and the cheque for the Probate Office fees should be made out to 'The Supreme Court Fees Account'.

Form PA1

In Northern Ireland, it is not necessary to serve a notice on an executor who is not acting and who has not renounced. It is therefore possible for one executor to obtain probate, without another executor even being aware that he or she is an executor.

Fees due for probate applications

Net estate under £10,000:	nil
Net estate between £10,000 and £25,000:	£75
Net estate between £25,000 and £40,000:	£145
Net estate between £40,000 and £70,000:	£260
Net estate between £70,000 and £100,000:	£330
Net estate between £100,000 and £200,000:	£410
For each additional £100,000 thereafter:	£65

 The website for the Probate and Matrimonial Office in Belfast is www.courtsni.gov.uk. The Royal Courts of Justice is also at www.courtsni.gov.uk. To contact the Londonderry District Probate Registry, telephone 028 7126 1832.

Transfer of a property

While property is registered or unregistered as in England and Wales, land law legislation generally in Northern Ireland is very different from that in England and Wales.

In the case of registered land, the executors or administrators complete assent **Form 17**. The completed Form 17 is then sent to the Land Registers of Northern Ireland in Belfast, together with the land certificate, the original grant of probate or letters of administration and **Form 100A** (Application for Registration). Both forms are available from the Land Registers (see below). The fee is £50. If the property is subject to a mortgage, the certificate of charge with the 'vacate' or receipt sealed by the bank or building society should be lodged at the same time, together with an additional fee of £25. Cheques should be made payable to 'DOE General Account'.

Unregistered land is, in fact, registered in the Registry of Deeds, held at the Land Registers. Although no particular form of words is required in order to vest property in a beneficiary, the wording varies both as to whether the title to the property is freehold, 'fee farm grant', or leasehold, and as to whether the property has been specifically bequeathed or forms part of the residue. In these cases, ask a solicitor to prepare an assent for unregistered land. The solicitor can arrange for a memorial of the assent to be registered in the Registry of Deeds, for which the Registry charges a fee of £14. The memorial is an extract of the assent giving the date, names of the parties executing the deed, the address of the property and whether the property is freehold or leasehold.

❝Wording varies on a title deed when land is unregistered. If you see the words 'fee farm grant', this means the property is freehold.❞

 The website for the Land Registers of Northern Ireland is www.lrni.gov.uk. Once you've registered on the website you have direct access to the Land Registers of Northern Ireland.

Distribution on intestacy

The main difference between English and Northern Irish law about wills and probate relates to the rules on intestacy. In Northern Ireland, unlike in England and Wales, no life interests are created on intestacy. As in England, the nearest relatives in a fixed order are entitled to apply for the grant of letters of administration (see page 171) and, if the nearest relative does not wish to be administrator, he or she can renounce the right to do so, in favour of the next nearest.

The surviving spouse normally becomes the administrator. Where there is a surviving spouse, he or she is always entitled to the deceased's personal effects, no matter how great their value. For all other circumstances of an intestate estate, consult a solicitor.

❝ Even for an intestate will, where there is a surviving spouse, he or she is always entitled to the deceased's personal effects. ❞

Winding up the estate

Applying for and receiving probate can take many months of preparation and correspondence, but by this stage the end is in sight. As soon as probate is granted all creditors can be paid, tax affairs finalised and beneficiaries given their dues.

The administration

This chapter describes what happens after the grant of probate.

GATHERING THE ASSETS

Enclosed with the probate will be the number of sealed copies of it that you requested. This enables you to proceed with the administration more quickly because instead of having to send the probate in turn to each organisation requiring to see it, you can send a copy to all interested parties at the same time. Write to each company or bank (see pages 147–63) sending the completed claim form and a copy of the sealed probate – and remember to ask for the probate to be returned once the details have been entered in their records, which is often referred to as 'registering the probate'.

As a rule, banks do not allow the credit on the deceased's bank account to be treated as available until probate is obtained. As a result, you may be faced with paying overdraft interest to a bank even though there is money available in the same bank, which will only be paid to the executor when probate has been granted.

Premium Bonds are not transferable and must be repaid, though the other National Savings products do not have to be encashed but can be simply transferred to beneficiaries after probate. On some types of National

Savings there is a limit to the total amount any one person is allowed to hold, but this limit can be exceeded if the excess is the result of transferring to the inheritor the savings held by the deceased. National Savings Certificates are exempt from income tax.

After you have followed up all the organisations, all the money due to the estate will be paid into the executorship account at your bank.

It is not advisable for the inexperienced to sell shares direct without a broker. When it is done through a bank, it is the bank's broker who does the actual selling. If a broker is used, find out his or her commission rates before giving dealing instructions. Selling through a bank's broker attracts a commission just as selling through any other broker does, often with a minimum fee of, say, £15 per holding. The bank may also charge a dealing fee.

PAYING OFF CREDITORS

Once there are no further assets to collect in, you need to pay all creditors before distributing the rest of the estate to the beneficiaries. During this time, you might want to consider putting some of the money, leaving enough to pay creditors, into a deposit account to earn more interest.

The most likely bills to be paid are:

- Funeral director
- A mortgage company
- Gas
- Electricity
- Telephone
- Credit card
- Any hire purchase agreements
- Income tax (see pages 186–7)
- and, if it takes more than six months from grant of probate to sell a property, council tax.

Finding unknown creditors

A personal representative is obliged to make full enquiries to discover what debts the deceased had. In addition, there is a procedure that involves advertising for creditors. After obtaining probate, put an advertisement in the *London Gazette* and a local newspaper announcing that all claims against the estate should be made by a certain date, which should be at least two months after the appearance of the advertisement. When this is done in the official way, you, as the personal representative, will be quite safe to distribute the assets of the estate on the basis of the

> ## Income Support
>
> If the deceased was receiving Income Support, contact the Benefits Agency as a refund may be due to the Agency if the deceased had not disclosed all his or her capital to it.

debts known to you on the date by which claims have to be made. Failure to do this could make you liable to pay creditors who apply for payment after you have paid the beneficiaries.

> **❝ Paying off creditors is a big step towards completion of your duties as executor. ❞**

> ## IHT rectification
>
> When there has been no agreement with the district valuer about the value of a house, the first contact with him or her is likely to be after probate has been obtained. Where this happens, the value of the house as finally agreed with the district valuer may be higher than the value included in the HM Revenue & Customs account. This results in a further payment of IHT having to be made at this stage for which you will need to fill in two copies of Form IHT 30 (see page box at foot of page 164 for details on obtaining), which fixes the value of assets conclusively as at the date of death. If the possible sale of a house is concerned, it may be prudent to wait, because then the question of value can be re-opened.

INCOME TAX RETURN

As an executor, there are now two questions to answer: first, is a tax return necessary to settle the tax affairs of the deceased up to the date of his or her death and, second, is a tax return necessary to deal with the income received by you during the administration of the estate?

" In some instances, the deceased may be owed a tax refund. "

The tax affairs of the deceased

Generally speaking, any income of the deceased received before his or her death should be included in a tax return. If the deceased has kept up to date with his or her tax returns and paid tax through PAYE, the final return prepared by the executors will usually have to cover only the period from 6 April before his or her death to the date of death. In some instances, however, depending on the date of death, two tax returns covering the last two tax years may have to be completed. The full amount of personal reliefs, however, will be available to set against the income and capital gains received or realised in that period. As a result, a refund of tax may be due.

Income received by the executors

Executors have to pay basic or lower-rate (20 per cent) tax on any income or 10 per cent on dividend income they receive. You then pay the remaining net income to the beneficiary with a certificate giving details of the tax that has already been paid on that income.

Although you do not receive any personal reliefs for income tax, you do not pay higher rate tax. However, there is one permitted deduction: if you had to take out a loan to pay IHT, the loan interest could be deducted. Technically, HM Revenue & Customs could object to a deduction of interest for probate fees, as opposed to IHT, but some inspectors do not take this view.

You are also liable for CGT on chargeable gains realised on the sale of assets (including houses) in the

 If you are in any doubt as to the calculation of a tax return, consult an accountant or get in touch with HM Revenue & Customs at www.hmrc.gov. uk for advice.

 For more information on Capital Gains Tax (CGT), see page 189. At this stage, it is worth double checking that you have contacted everyone that you initially got in touch with, as outlined on pages 147-58.

estate. In this case, you are allowed the same exemption as an individual for the year in which the deceased died, and the following two years (then no exemption in subsequent years), although the rate of tax is now 40 per cent.

Where an asset is passed direct to a beneficiary (rather than being sold by the estate), the beneficiary acquires the asset at its value at the date of death. If the beneficiary subsequently sells, they are liable for CGT based on their own allowance and tax rate. Therefore, when you are considering whether to distribute assets or cash from their sale, you might want to consider whether more or less tax would be paid according to whether any assets were sold by the estate or by a beneficiary.

THE DISTRIBUTION

Once all the debts are settled and the tax paid, you are free to distribute the assets in accordance with the will. Some of the assets can be handed over directly to the beneficiaries, in return for a receipt. Other assets, such as shares and a house, if they are not being sold, have to be transferred by deed or other document to the beneficiary. There is also the question of expenses.

Expenses

All the expenses involved in the administration of the estate will be paid out of the executorship account at the bank. These expenses might include:

- **The cost of the probate** and obtaining copies of it
- **The bank's charge** on the transfer of shares and the Land Registry fees relating to the transfer of a house
- **Your out-of-pocket expenses,** such as postage and fares to visit the Probate Registry. Personal representatives are not entitled to be paid for the time they devote to the administration of the estate, unless the will specifically says so.

Legacies

Any legacies can also now be paid although a legacy for a person under 18 cannot be paid directly to that child. The executors, therefore, have to invest the money until each child, on becoming 18, can receive his or her share (plus the interest it had earned meanwhile). You might also want to consult an independent investment adviser on how best to invest a legacy

Paying legacies

Wills usually provide that a legacy is clear of tax (which then comes out of the residue unless the legacy is tax free). However, the actual wording must be checked. Interest at an appropriate rate can be claimed if the executor has not paid the legacy within one year of the death. The executor should take care to get a receipt.

to comply with the proviso of the Trustee Act 2000.

When an administration is long and complicated, it is possible that the legacies will not be paid for several years. When the legacy is then paid, the legatee is entitled not only to the actual amount of the legacy but also to interest (currently at 6 per cent per annum) from the date one year after the date of death until payment of the legacy. This is taxable as income in the hands of the recipient, but it is deductible against any income earned in the administration for income tax purposes.

Shares

It is often necessary to sell some or all of the shares held by a person who has died in order to pay the debts, IHT or the legacies or to meet the expenses of administering the estate. When this happens, it is then the remaining shares that are divided according to the will.

When shares or unit trust holdings are sold within a year of a death for less than the value on the date of death, the total of the gross selling price of all such investments can be substituted as the value for IHT. The sale has to be made by the executors, but once the shares have been transferred into the names of the beneficiaries, it is too late to claim a reduction of IHT. Adjustment is made by a corrective document. Where the market for shares has fallen generally, this can be a valuable relief if some shares have to be sold.

Whether the shares are sold or not, it is necessary for each company in which shares are held to see a copy of the probate (see box at foot of page 155 for finding a registrar's address). In a case where a sole executor is also the person entitled to the shares under the will, the company will usually provide its own form in order to complete the transfer. Whether the shares are to be sold or transferred direct to the beneficiaries entitled to have them under the will, it is usually possible to send the

Dividing Shares

If shares remain unsold and they are passed on to beneficiaries, it is possible to divide each existing holding between them, equally or otherwise - always get a written confirmation of the division from the interested parties. If no agreement is possible, all the shares should be sold and the beneficiaries should get their entitlement in cash. Then there can be no argument about who gets what, but from an investment point of view this may not be the most advantageous thing to do.

To effect a division, you can employ the bank or stockbroker. All they will need are the holding certificates, and any fees (ranging from nothing to between £2 and £6 per share) will be debited from the executorship account.

probate to the registrar of the company at the same time as sending the transfers of the shares to be dealt with by him or her.

Transfer of a property

Where a mortgage is outstanding at the time of death and there is nothing in the will about having it paid off out of the residue, the house may have to be sold so that the mortgage can be repaid from the proceeds of the sale and the beneficiaries would get the balance of the money. However, many people nowadays have a mortgage protection policy or a mortgage backed by an endowment policy, so that the mortgage can be repaid automatically on the death of the borrower.

Be very careful what the will says if a property with a mortgage is left to a beneficiary. Does the will say that the mortgage is to be repaid from the residue or is the gift made subject to the mortgage?

Where the house is going to be transferred outright into the name of a beneficiary, the building society may be prepared to let the beneficiary continue with the existing mortgage. He or she can, of course, apply to any source – another building society or bank, for example – for a new mortgage if that gives a better deal.

❝If a mortgage is outstanding, the house may have to be sold so that the mortgage can be repaid.❞

The title of the house will also have to be transferred to the beneficiary. Contact the mortgage company or Land Registry for advice on how to do this. There will be different procedures to follow depending on whether or not the property is registered at the Land Registry.

CAPITAL GAINS TAX

Capital gains can arise when assets are sold or transferred for more than they cost when they were bought or more than their probate value (that is, their value at the time of the owner's death). Take professional advice as to how to minimise CGT.

 Where there are any complications, such as restrictive covenants on the property, take legal advice to make sure that, as executor, you are not left with any personal liability.

 For the Which? report on captial gains tax, go to the Which? website: www.which.co.uk. Some of the content on the website is only available to subscribers – information for how to subscribe is given on the website.

FINAL STEPS

Once all the debts have been paid, there are no outstanding claims and all other property has been distributed, all that remains is to distribute the remaining cash. Before doing this, though, personal representatives should consider carefully everything they have done on the account.

Double check every asset in the estate and look at each debt and expense to see that everything has been done properly. This is important if several people are sharing the residue, and it would be more important still if there had been any dissent within the family. Ask any fellow executor to look over the papers, too. Once you are happy with everything, prepare the estate accounts.

Accounts

These accounts don't have to take any particular form as long as they are clear and accurate (for an example, see page 192–3). It is useful to have a separate note of the income received, so that the calculation of the tax credit due to each beneficiary is more straightforward.

The final balance on the accounts should match the closing balance at the bottom of the last bank statement. If these figures are not the same, something is wrong, and you then have to look at everything – starting with the adding-up.

It is, of course, unlikely that the values of all the assets shown in the IHT 200 or IHT 205 at the date of death will match exactly the money received when the accounts are closed or transferred. Interest will have accrued and shares may have risen or fallen in value.

Some estate accounts show the value of the assets at the date of

 The webiste for HM Revenue & Customs is www.hmrc.gov.uk where you can download most of their forms.

death and then the transactions taking place during the administration.

Send a copy of the accounts to each of the beneficiaries for their approval, asking them to sign and return the accounts to you. At the same time, you can send the cheques for the final amount owing together with an R185 form, if necessary (see box, opposite), and ask each recipient to sign a formal acknowledgement. If you are worried that a beneficiary might challenge the accounts, you could arrange for them to be professionally audited as a precaution.

When the cheques are cleared, you can close the executors' account, although there may be a small amount of residue left to distribute after closuer because interest accrues to the last day. The administration is now finished. Bundle together all the papers, including the original probate and the signed copy of the accounts, and put them in a large envelope to be kept in a safe place, theoretically for 12 years (where there are any life interests under any trusts in the will, the papers should then be kept for 12 years after final distribution following the death of anyone with a life interest). The probate could be kept as a family document.

❝ If you are worried that a beneficiary might challenge the accounts, you could always arrange for them to be professionally audited. ❞

Example of how the final accounts might look

CAPITAL ACCOUNT

Assets

Property	227,500.00
Endowment policy	85,300.00
Life policy	9,100.00
Building Society	81,000.00
Bank	1,900.00
National Savings Certificates	5,000.00
Premium Bonds	4,000.00
1,500 units Investment Fund (sold)	2,730.00
£50,000 5% Treasury Stock 2008 (sold)	51,000.00
Retained shares	85,550.00
Jewellery (valued)	1,500.00
Car (estimated)	4,000.00
Contents (estimated)	11,000.00
Private pension arrears	200.00
State benefit arrears	78.00
Cash	80.00
	569,938.00

Liabilities

Funeral account		2,200.00
Household bills		320.00
Mortgage on a property		25,400.00
Probate fees		140.00
Executor's expenses		200.00
Land Registry fees		70.00
Guarantee for missing shares		35.00
Inheritance tax (1st payment)	69,816.83	
payment on a property	40.948.77	
final adjustment	960.00	111,725.60
Balance transferred to distribution account		429,847.40
		569,938.00

INCOME ACCOUNT

Received	Tax	Net
Building society (after 8/4)	25.00	100.00
Dividend from shares (after 8/4)	44.00	396.00
Interest – executor's bank account	7.50	30.00
Transfer to distribution account	76.50	526.00

THE DISTRIBUTION ACCOUNT

Received

Balance from Capital Account made up as follows:

Any property	227,500.00	
Retained shares	85,550.00	
Jewellery	1,500.00	
Car	4,000.00	
Contents	11,000.00	
Cash balance	100,297.40	
		429,847.40
Balance from income account		526.00
		430,373.40

Distribution

Legacies e.g. grandchildren (£500 each)	1,500.00
– a charity	100.00
1st beneficiary: a car	4,000.00
the contents of a property	11,000.00
a property	227,500.00
The residue: 2nd beneficiary: 1/2 shares (value)	42,775.00
1/2 balance	50,361.70
3rd beneficiary: 1/2 shares (value)	42,775.00
1/2 balance (including jewellery, valued at £1,500)	50,361.70
	430,373.40

In the capital account, include the capital balance in the building society account at the date of death and interest accrued to that date. The income account includes any interest accrued after the date of death. The other interest payment represents the further interest due to the date of closing of the executor's deposit account.

In the income account, include the receipts of all the income received after the date of death, so they are excluded from the capital account to avoid recording the same item twice.

Problems and disputes

It is a sad fact that the death of a family member can trigger a dispute within the family. The first sign of trouble is often preceded by the remark 'It's not the money that I'm bothered about. It's the principle of the matter.' Another sad fact is that the cost of a dispute can reach astronomical levels and consume the value of the estate that is in dispute.

However, disputes do arise and have to be dealt with. They fall into two main categories. First, there are disputes over the will. Was it valid? Was it fair? Was it forged? Second, disputes can arise over the administration of the estate of the deceased person. Are the executors or administrators acting improperly or failing to do what they should be doing? Have they paid out to the wrong person or are they refusing to tell the beneficiaries what they have done? This section first deals with both kinds of problems, and then discusses other common issues.

If you are involved in a dispute over a will or administration, the best advice you will get is to try to settle it as quickly as possible, and perhaps to have a word with the Probate Registry (see below). If that cannot be done, you will almost certainly need to instruct a solicitor who knows his or her way around court procedures.

❝ If you are involved in a dispute over a will or its administration, try to settle it as quickly as possible. The next step would be to instruct a solicitor. ❞

To contact the Probate Registry, go to www.courtservice.gov.uk. Their helpline phone number is 0845 302 0900, and there are plenty of articles on the website that might address your particular problem.

PROBLEMS WITH THE WILL

Executors responsible for an estate and getting probate for it before distribution to the beneficiaries are strictly regulated by law. They also commonly face problems which can impede progress and can also mean, at the worst, that the rules of intestacy apply.

No will can be found

The deceased person may never have made a will, but what if one of the family believes that he or she did make one and it cannot be found? If a thorough search of papers and possessions fails to discover the will, one step is to write to local firms of solicitors and banks who might have been employed to make or keep a will on the deceased's behalf. If all enquiries fail, the rules of intestacy apply.

Was it signed properly?

The will should be carefully checked to ensure that it has been signed by the testator and that the testator's signature has been witnessed by two witnesses (who must not be beneficiaries to the will). Both witnesses must have been present when the will was signed. As executor, if you have any doubts about the signing of the will, check with the witnesses. If the will has not been properly signed and witnessed, the Probate Registrar may declare it invalid or at the very least require a sworn affidavit to explain the irregularity.

Was the will dated?

If it is not dated, you have a problem. Do the witnesses remember when it was signed? If so, the Probate Registry will require an affidavit to explain the lack of a date. Sometimes, it is apparent that a will has been changed or that some other document has been attached. Take all the documentation you have to the Probate Registrar, who can advise whether any of it should be counted as part of the will.

Is it the last will?

Even if you find a will that is properly dated and witnessed, it may not necessarily be the last will the deceased made. The older the will, the greater the chance that a later will or a codicil exists changing its terms. Always make further enquiries to be sure. Remember, too, that even an apparently valid will may have been wholly or partly invalidated by a subsequent marriage or divorce.

Remarriage automatically revokes any earlier will unless that will was specifically stated to be made in contemplation of the marriage. In particular, if there are children and a new will wasn't made folowing a remarriage, the rules of intestacy will automatically operate after death.

PROBLEMS WITH THE TESTATOR
Did the testator have 'testamentary capacity'?

In order to make a valid will, a testator must understand what he or she owns, understand the effect of the will and recognise individuals to whom he or she might have responsibilities – for instance, a wife with young children. As executor, if you believe the testator lacked testamentary capacity, you need medical evidence to support your case and should take legal advice.

> **"Probate actions can be very expensive, transferring a large proportion of the estate to the solicitor and barristers involved."**

Was the testator threatened or improperly influenced?

Anyone wishing to challenge the will on these grounds must show that the testator was induced to make it by force, fear or fraud or that in some other way the will was not made voluntarily. Legal advice should be taken before attempting to challenge a will on these grounds.

If someone decides to challenge the will, he or she may apply to the Probate Registry for a 'caveat'. This prevents an application for probate being made. It covers all registries and lasts for six months. If not renewed, it lapses. While it is in force, probate cannot be issued. If a caveat has been registered, as executor, you first have to resolve the problem with the applicant. If you cannot, you have to issue a warning to the Probate Registry, which has the effect of beginning a court action to settle the dispute. This is an area requiring specialist knowledge, so seek legal advice at an early stage.

Is the will or distribution on intestacy unfair?

If it is generally agreed by the beneficiaries that the will (or intestacy) has not made reasonable provision for all the interested parties, they can enter into a 'post-death variation'. This has the effect of rewriting the will or intestacy rules. This step must be taken within two years of the death. If the variation reduces the share of a beneficiary who is under 18, the court's approval must be obtained. If you wish to make such an agreement, take legal advice. If there is no agreement and the matter remains in dispute, the only recourse is to take the dispute to court. Probate actions can be very expensive, in effect transferring a substantial proportion of the estate from the beneficiaries to their solicitors and barristers. If there is no alternative, the claimant has to take proceedings under the Inheritance (Provision for Family and Dependants) Act 1975.

OTHER PROBLEMS WITH WILLS
Bankrupt beneficiaries

If you suspect that a beneficiary is bankrupt, you should make further enquiries, including a search on form K16 at the Land Charges Registry. Any payments due to a bankrupt must be made to his or her trustee in bankruptcy who must produce an S.307 notice under the Insolvency Act 1986.

Missing beneficiaries

If you have to find beneficiaries, use what detective qualities you have. In addition to family networks and newspaper advertisements, you could use the internet to track down missing people. Genealogists can be engaged for intractable problems on a 'no-find no-fee' basis – check that their finding fee is a reasonable proportion of the sum involved. Another solution, if the circumstances are appropriate, is to obtain a court order permitting distribution or to pay the money into court under the provisions of S.63 if the Trustee Act 1925.

Problem executors or administrators

If it appears that a personal representative is unsuitable or is failing to carry out his or her duties, an application for removal can be made to the High Court. Before doing so, it is wise to ask the Probate Registrar or a solicitor with specific experience for advice.

Claims by ex-spouses, dependants and family members

If there is an ex-spouse to whom maintenance is still being paid following a divorce or separation, he or she is entitled to make a claim against the estate, so remember to take this possibility into account. The extent of the claim will depend upon the size of the estate and the other claimants. Similarly, a cohabitee or child of the deceased who considers the will to be unfair can make a claim against the estate under the provisions of the Inheritance (Provision for Family and Dependants) Act 1975. Under the Act, the claimant has to file a claim no later than six months after the grant of probate or letters of administration. If there is any risk of a claim being made, executors should limit any distribution made during that six-month period.

Having the right to claim does not mean that a person automatically wins the case if a claim is made, especially where the applicant has not been dependent on the deceased. Legal costs of the action are a matter for the court

For an outline of the rules of intestacy, see pages 171-2, which might help throw light on your particular case.

to decide. Such a person is not paid automatically by the estate nor are the costs paid automatically from the estate.

Court of Protection

If the affairs of the person who has died have been administered by the Court of Protection (in cases of mental illness, for example), there are formalities to go through with the court before the assets of the deceased can come under the control of the personal representatives. This usually requires the 'receiver' to file final accounts at the Court of Protection but, if all parties agree, that requirement can be waived. The receiver is the person appointed by the court to look after the financial affairs of people who cannot look after themselves, known as 'patients'.

Foreign property

Generally speaking, if a deceased person owned property or land in

 Other probate disputes can end up in the High Court or in the Chancery Division. In either case the proceedings will be costly and you will need advice. Neither court is DIY territory.

another country, the laws there determine what happens to the property at death and overrule what is said in the English or Welsh will. Seek advice from a solicitor with specific knowledge of the relevant law of the country involved. The Law Society can provide names of suitable solicitors.

Foreign domicile

If the deceased person had a foreign domicile (that is, the country which was recognised as his or her permanent home), the law of the country of domicile applies to the administration of the estate although probate (or letters of administration) will be required to deal with English and Welsh property owned by such a person.

Caveats and citations

If you wish to prevent the issue of a grant of probate because you believe the will is invalid or that the applicant has no right to apply, you may file a caveat at the Probate Registry. This prevents probate being issued while the problem is resolved. If you simply want to know when probate is issued, you should make a standing search. If the caveat is challenged by a warning, that has the effect of commencing a probate action.

 For advice about buying a home overseas, see the Which? Essential Guide *Buying Property Abroad*.

Pensions and other benefits

Following the death of a spouse or close relative, you may become eligible for certain payments from the state. As well as covering bereavement benefits, married couple's allowance and pensions, this sections tells you other state benefits, including income support.

The Department for Work and Pensions (DWP) administers all Social Security benefits. Explanatory leaflets for different categories of people – for example, on bereavement benefits – are available without charge at any local Social Security office or Jobcentre Plus office or from the Pension Service when you are over working age. It is crucial to note that these leaflets are updated at irregular intervals and the information contained in them may change considerably from one edition to another; new leaflets are also produced (see also page 203).

Some benefits are paid only to the dependants of those who had paid, or had credited to them, National Insurance contributions during their lifetime. You are not expected to know what contributions have been paid or credited when you apply for any benefits. The HM Revenue & Customs Contributions Office keeps records of everyone's contributions. The number of contributions required varies according to the type of benefit claimed. When the number of contributions does not qualify for the full amount of certain benefits, a reduced rate may be paid.

BEREAVEMENT BENEFITS

There are three benefits that you may be entitled to if your husband or wife dies. They are:

- **Bereavement payment:** a tax-free payment of £2,000 paid to you as soon as you are widowed.
- **Widowed parent's allowance:** a taxable weekly benefit.
- **Bereavement allowance:** a taxable weekly benefit paid for 52 weeks after your husband or wife dies, if you are aged 45 or over.

The Department for Work and Pensions is contacted via www.dwp.gov.uk and to find your local Jobcentre Plus office, go to www.jobcentreplus.gov.uk. HM Revenue & Customs is at www.hmrc.gov.uk.

Death abroad

If you need to find out more about claiming any benefits after someone has died abroad, contact the International Pension Centre (www.thepensionservice.gov.uk).

To qualify for the benefits, your husband or wife must have paid the required number of National Insurance (NI) contributions – your own NI contributions do not count. These new benefits are available to both widows and widowers. Previously, only women were eligible for bereavement benefits.

You need to have been married at the time of death to qualify – you will not be entitled to claim if you are divorced. You also lose your entitlement if you remarry or live with someone else as husband and wife as if you are married to them.

You can make a claim for bereavement benefits on Form BB1, available from any Social Security office or from the DWP. Leaflet GL14 is also available from the DWP and is a basic guide to benefits and tax for women and men who have been widowed. Both documents can be downloaded from the DWP website.

You will need to complete details of your marriage, pension and any dependent children on the form. To qualify you will need to send the death certificate, your birth certificate and marriage certificate, birth certificates for dependent children and your spouse's retirement pension order book with Form BB1.

You should claim the bereavement benefits as soon as possible to make sure you do not lose any of the benefits. Payments cannot normally be backdated for more than three months from the date of the application. Claimants should not delay if they are waiting for probate, which may take several months, but make an initial claim as soon as possible. When you make the application you can choose how any benefits are paid – either with a book of weekly orders or straight into a bank account.

MARRIED COUPLE'S ALLOWANCE

Married couple's allowance was abolished with effect from April 2000. You will be able to claim only if the person who dies was born before 6 April 1935 (i.e. if the deceased was 65 before 6 April 2000). If you think you might be entitled to married couple's allowance, contact HM Revenue & Customs.

❝Claim your bereavement benefits as soon as you possibly can to make sure you don't lose out.❞

If your wife dies, you can continue to receive the married couple's allowance for the whole of the tax year during which your wife dies. If part or all of the allowance had been allocated to your wife, you can have any unused part transferred to you.

WAR WIDOW'S PENSION
A widow whose husband had been in the armed forces should contact the Veterans Agency Helpline (see below), explaining the circumstances and asking if she is entitled to a war widow's pension.

STATE SECOND PENSION
In April 2002, the State Second Pension (S2P) replaced the State Earnings-Related Pension Scheme (SERPS). Both S2P and SERPS are paid in addition to any state retirement pension that is payable. For more information, see www.direct.gov.uk or www.thepensionservice.gov.uk.

OTHER STATE BENEFITS
If your income and savings are below certain levels you may be able to claim benefits to top up your income. Advice can be obtained from agencies such as the Citizens Advice Bureau, as well as Social Security or Jobcentre Plus offices.

Income Support
If you don't work, or work for less than 16 hours a week, and your savings total less than £8,000, you can claim Income Support (known as Minimum Income Guarantee if you are over 60) if your weekly income is below a specified amount. This varies depending on your circumstances, i.e. your age, whether you have dependent children and, if so, how old they are, whether you have a disability or suffer from a chronic illness, whether you have a mortgage to pay and so on.

Child Tax Credit and Working Tax Credit
From April 2003, Children's Tax Credit, Working Families Tax Credit and Disabled Person's Tax Credit were replaced by two new credits:

Child Tax Credit: a tax credit for people with children up to 16 years old (or under 19 if in full-time education).
Working Tax Credit: a tax credit to top up the earnings of people on low incomes, including those who do not have children.

To receive one or both credits you need to claim via the HM Revenue & Customs website, or by phoning

 The Veterans Agency Helpline is contacted at www.veteransagency.mod.uk, the Pension Service is at www.pensionservice.gov.uk and the Citizens Advice Bureau website is www.adviceguide.org.uk.

(0845) 300 3900 and asking for claim form TC600.

The new tax credit system may seem complicated – but do not be put off. You will not get them unless you apply for them. For more information, see the HM Revenue & Customs website: www.hmrc.org.uk.

Pension Credit

Pension Credits are a new system for topping up pensioners' incomes. People aged 60 or over could claim extra money to guarantee them a minimum income. People over 65 years who have modest savings or investments, or income from a second pension or annuity, may also be entitled to extra money. To apply, contact the Pension Service.

Child Benefit

If you are bringing up a child, you can claim Child Benefit even if you are not the parent. Child Benefit is not affected by income or savings, and you need to claim in your name for each child under 16 or 19 if in full-time education.

Health costs

If you are claiming Income Support, Income-based Jobseeker's Allowance, Pension Credit or Working Tax Credit, you may be able to get help with health costs. If not, you may get help through the NHS low income scheme.

Housing Benefit and Council Tax Benefit

If your savings are less than £16,000 and your income is below a certain amount (which varies according to your circumstances), you may be able to claim Housing Benefit to help you pay your rent and Council Tax. Claim forms and information are available from local council offices, for example leaflets GL16 'Help with Your Rent' and GL17 'Help with Your Council Tax'. All these are obtainable from Social Security, DWP and Jobcentre Plus.

❝Child Benefit is not affected by income or savings and you need to claim in your name.❞

Jobseeker's Allowance

If you are unemployed, over 18 and less than 65 for men and 60 for women, capable of, available and actively seeking work, you may be eligible to receive Jobseeker's Allowance. If enough National Insurance contributions have been paid, you may be able to get Contribution-based Jobseeker's Allowance; if not, you may be eligible for Income-based Jobseeker's Allowance. In addition, if you qualify for a free element of pension credit, you automatically get full council tax benefit. For further information, see leaflet IR41, available from HM Revenue & Customs or Jobcentre Plus.

Guardian's Allowance

A person who takes an orphaned child into the family may be entitled to a Guardian's Allowance. Although the payment is called a Guardian's Allowance, it is not necessary to assume legal guardianship to qualify. Usually the allowance is paid only when both parents are dead, but it can sometimes be paid after the death of one parent – for instance, where the other is missing or cannot be traced or is detained in prison or hospital, or where the parents were divorced (and certain conditions apply). The allowance is not awarded unless one of the child's parents was born in the UK or had been resident in the UK for a specified length of time, or is a national or member of a family of an EU country and insured under UK Social Security legislation. It is paid only if the guardian qualifies for child benefit for the child.

Claims for the allowance should be made on Form BG1, obtainable from the DWP or Jobcentre Plus. A claim should be made straight away as you may lose your benefit if you delay (it can be backdated only for up to three months or to the date of the award of Child Benefit).

Changes at short notice

The government, the DWP and HM Revenue & Customs may make substantial changes to benefits and the qualifications for them at short notice. The information given here is accurate at the time of writing (2006), but if you are considering claiming any benefits or tax credits, contact your local Social Security office, Jobcentre Plus office, the DWP or HM Revenue & Customs to get accurate and up-to-date information and advice. You should also make sure you have the latest edition of any leaflet, and ask if anything has changed since it was published. You may lose some benefits if you do not do this.

Glossary

Administration of the estate: The task of the executor or administrator.

Administrator: The name given to a personal representative if not appointed by a valid will. The administrator will usually have to obtain letters of administration to show that he or she is the person with legal authority to deal with the property of the deceased.

Attesting registrar: An interim register office, which passes all relevant information to the receiving registrar.

Bequest: A gift of a particular object or cash (as opposed to 'devise', which means land or buildings).

Book of Remembrance: Popular means of memorial at a crematorium.

CGT: Capital Gains Tax.

Certificate for cremation: Certificate issued by a coroner if a post mortem has been ordered – 'Form E'.

Certificate of no liability to register: A registrar's certificate, issued under certain circumstances such as a death overseas, confirming that a death is not required to be registered.

Chattels: Personal belongings: for example, jewellery, furniture, wine, pictures, books, even cars and horses not used for business. Does not include money or investments.

Child (referred to in a will or intestacy): Child of the deceased including adopted and illegitimate children but, unless specifically included in a will, not stepchildren.

Citation: A document issued by the Registry (upon application) calling on a person to explain why he or she has not taken a certain step, for example, why has there been no application for probate if that person is shown in the will to be an executor.

Co-habitee: A partner of the deceased who may be able to claim a share of the estate. The term 'common law wife' has no legal force.

Columbarium: A niche in a wall at a crematorium where ashes can be walled in or left in an urn.

Common grave: When the burial authority has the right to bury another person in the same plot.

Confirmation the document issued to executors by the sheriff court in Scotland to authorise them to administer the estate.

Deed of grant: Confirms the existence of a private grave (see exclusive right of burial).

Demise: a grant of a lease.

District valuer: The district valuer is employed by HM Revenue & Customs but the job has little to do with taxes as such. He or she is concerned with the valuation of land, houses, factories, shops, offices and so on for many official purposes. He or she is an expert on valuation.

Estate: All the assets and property of the deceased, including houses, cars, investments, money and personal belongings.

Exclusive right of burial: When a plot is leased for x number of years.

Executor: The name given to a personal representative if he or she is appointed by a valid will or codicil. The executor will usually have to apply for probate of the will to show that he or she is the person with legal authority to deal with the property of the deceased.

Executor-dative: An administrator appointed by court for a person who dies intestate.

Executor-nominate: The Scottish term for the English term 'executor'.

Faculty: Special application to the church authorities for reserving a grave.

Family grave: A specific grave where only members of the family can be buried.

First offices: When a funeral director prepares a body for burial of cremation.

Form BD8: A free form supplied by the registrar for claiming Social Security benefits.

Grant of probate: The document issued by the probate registry to the executors of a will to authorise them to administer the estate.

Green certificate: The official certificate provided by the registrar authorising a burial or cremation to take place.

Hypostasis: When someone has been dead for half an hour or more, parts of the skin begin to discolour with purple/black patches. It is also known as post mortem (meaning 'after death' – nothing to do with post mortem examinations) staining, and is due to blood settling in parts of the body due because of gravity.

Informant: The person who registers a death.

Inheritance tax (IGT): The tax that may be payable when the total estate of the deceased person exceeds a set threshold (subject to various exemptions and adjustments).

Intestate: A person who dies without making a will.

Issue: All the lineal descendants of a person, that is, children, grandchildren, great-grandchildren and so on.

Last offices: When a nurse prepares a body in hospital for burial of cremation.

Lawn grave: When grave consists of a headstone with mown grass around it.

Laying out: The initial preparation of a body for burial or cremation.

Legacy: A gift of money.

Letters of administration: The document issued by the probate registry to the administer the estate of an intestate.

Letters of administration with will annexed: The document issued by the probate registry to the administrator when there is a will but the will does not deal with everything e.g. it fails to appoint an executor.

Mausoleum: A large, brick-built construction.

Minor: A person under 18 years of age.

Moveable estate: Property other than land and buildings in Scotland.

Next of kin: The person entitled to the estate when a person dies intestate.

Letters of administration: The document issued to administrators by a probate registry to authorise them to administer the estate of an intestate.

Order for burial: Certificate issued by a coroner if a post mortem has been ordered.

Personal estate or personalty: All the investments and belongings of a person apart from land and buildings.

Personal representative: A general term for both administrators and executors.

Plaque Panel: A small notice with the name and date of death of the deceased, placed near a memorial rosebush or shrub or attached to a panel on a wall in the crematorium grounds.

Probate of the will: The document issued to executors by a probate registry in England, Wales and Northern Ireland to authorise them to administer the estate.

Proving the will: Making the application for probate to a probate registry.

Probate registry: The government office which deals with probate matters. The Principal Probate Registry is in London with district registries in cities and some large towns.

Real estate or realty: Land and buildings owned by a person.

Receiving registrar: The register office where the death must be registered. It must be in the sub-district in which the death took place or where the body was found.

Residue: What is left of the estate to share out after all the debts and specific bequests and legacies have been paid.

Rigor mortis: A stiffening of the muscles, which usually begins within about six hours after death and gradually extends over the whole body in about 24 hours; after this it usually begins to wear off. Rigor mortis is less pronounced in the body of an elderly person.

Solvent: Value of the assets exceeeds any debts.

Specific bequests, particular items gifted by will. They may be referred to as 'specific legacies'.

Testator: A person who makes a will.

Will: The document in which you say what is to happen to your possessions on your death.

Useful addresses

Age Concern England
Astral House
1268 London Road
Norbury
London SW16 4ER
Tel: 020 8679 8000
Information line: (0800) 009 966
www.ageconcern.org.uk

Age Concern Funeral Plan
Tel: 0800 731 0651

Age Concern Northern Ireland
3 Lower Crescent
Belfast BT7 1NR
Tel: 028 9024 5729
www.ageconcernni.org

Age Concern Scotland
113 Rose Street
Edinburgh EH2 3DT
Tel: 0131 220 3345
Information line: 0800 009 966
www.ageconcernscotland.org.uk

Age Concern Wales
4th Floor
1 Cathedral Road
Cardiff CF11 9SD
Tel: 029 2037 1566
www.accymru.org.uk

Asian Funeral Service
209 Kenton Road
Harrow
Middlesex HA3 0HD
Tel: 020 8909 3737

Association of Burial Authorities
Waterloo House
155 Upper Street
London N1 1RA
Tel: 020 7288 2522

Association of Charity Officers
Unicorn House
Station Close
Potters Bar EN6 3JW
Tel: 01707 651777
www.aco.uk.net

Benefits Agency
Look in your local phone book

Bereavement Register
Tel: 0870 600 7222
www.the-bereavement-register.com

Britannia Shipping Company for Burial
at Sea Ltd
Unit 3
The Old Sawmills
Hawkerland Road
Collaton Raleigh
Sidmouth
Devon EX10 0HP
Tel: 01395 568652

British Humanist Association
1 Gower Street
London WC1E 6HD
Tel: 020 7079 3580
www.humanism.org.uk

British Organ Donor Society (BODY)
Balsham
Cambridge CB1 6DL
Tel: 01223 893636
www.argonet.co.uk/body

Central Wills Directory
PO Box 108
East Grinstead
West Sussex RH19 2YY
Tel: 01342 302602
www.willsdirectory.com

Citizens Advice Bureau
Look in your local phone book or go to
www.adviceguide.org.uk

Commonwealth War Graves Commission
2 Marlow Road
Maidenhead
Berkshire SL6 7DX
Tel: 01628 634221
www.cwgc.org

Compassionate Friends
53 North Street
Bristol BS3 1EN
Helpline: 08451 232304
Tel: 08451 203785
www.tcf.org.uk

Cremation Society of Great Britain
2nd Floor
Brecon House
16–16a Albion Place
Maidstone ME14 5DZ
Tel: 01622 688292/3
www.cremation.org.uk

Cruse Bereavement Care
Cruse House
126 Sheen Road
Richmond TW9 1UR
Helpline: 0870 167 1677
Tel: 020 8939 9530
www.crusebereavementcare.org.uk

Department for Work and Pensions
(DWP)
Correspondence Unit, Room 112
The Adelphi
1–11 John Adam Street
London WC2N 6HT
Tel: 020 7712 2171
www.dwp.gov.uk

Department of Health Publications
PO Box 777
London SE1 6XH
Tel: 08701 555455
www.dh.gov.uk

Department of National Savings
Blackpool
FY3 9YP
Tel: 0845 964 5000
www.nationalsavings.co.uk

District Probate Registry
Court House
Bishop Street
Londonderry BT48 7PY
Tel: 028 7126 1832
For people living in Londonderry (Derry),
Fermanagh and Tyrone

Driver and Vehicle Licensing Agency
(DVLA)
Swansea SA1 1AA
Tel: 0870 240 0009
www.dvla.gov.uk

The Federation of British Cremation
Authorities
41 Salisbury Road
Carshalton
Surrey SM5 3HA
Tel: 020 8669 4521
www.fbca.org.uk

Foreign and Commonwealth Office (FCO)
Consular Division
Nationality and Passport Section
Old Admiralty Building
Whitehall, London SW1A 2AF
Tel: 020 7270 1500
www.fco.gov.uk

Foundation for the Study of Infant
Deaths (FSID)
11-19 Artillery Row
London SW1P 1RT
Helpline: 0870 787 0554
Tel: 0870 787 0855
www.sids.org.uk/fsid

Funeral Planning Authority (FPA)
Knellstone House
Udimore
Rye
East Sussex TN31 6AR
Tel: 0845 601 9619
www.funeralplanningauthority.com

Funeral Planning Council (FPC)
Melville House
70 Drymen Road
Bearsden
Glasgow G61 2RP
Tel: 0141 942 5855
www.golden-charter.co.uk

General Register Office
PO Box 2
Southport
Merseyside PR8 2JD
Tel: 0845 603 7788
www.gro.gov.uk

General Register Office for
Scotland
New Register House
3 West Register Street
Edinburgh EH1 3YT
Tel: 0131-314 4446
www.gro-scotland.gov.uk

Help the Aged
Head Office
207-221 Pentonville Road
London N1 9UZ
Tel: 020 7278 1114
www.helptheaged.org.uk

HM Revenue & Customs
Probate helpline: 0845 302 0900
Look in the phone book or use the
website for your local tax office or HM
Revenue & Customs Centre
www.hmrc.gov.uk

Home Office
Direct Communications Unit
2 Marsham Street
London SW1P 4DF
Tel: 020 7035 4848
www.homeoffice.gov.uk

INQUEST
89-93 Fonthill Road
London N4 3JH
Tel: 020 7263 1111
www.inquest.org.uk

Institute of Family Therapy
24-32 Stephenson Way
London NW1 2HX
Tel: 020-7391 9150
www.instituteoffamilytherapy.org.uk

International Pension Centre
Tyneview Park
Newcastle-upon-Tyne NE98 1BE
Tel: 0191 218 7777
www.thepensionservice.gov.uk

Jewish Bereavement Counselling Service
8-10 Forty Avenue
Wembley
Middlesex HA9 8JW
Tel: 020 8385 1874
www.jvisit.org.uk

Land Registers of Northern Ireland
Lincoln Building
27–45 Great Victoria Street
Belfast BT2 7SL
Tel: 028 9025 1555
www.lrni.gov.uk

Land Registry
32 Lincoln's Inn Fields
London WC2A 3PH
Tel: 020 7917 8888
www.landregistry.gov.uk

Law Society of England and Wales
Law Society Hall
113 Chancery Lane
London WC2A 1PL
Tel: 020 7242 1222
www.lawsociety.org.uk

Law Society of Northern Ireland
Law Society House
98 Victoria Street
Belfast BT1 3JZ
Tel: 028 9023 1614
www.lawsoc-ni.org

Law Society of Scotland
26 Drumsheugh Gardens
Edinburgh EH3 7YR
Tel: 0131 226 7411
www.lawscot.org.uk

Macmillan Cancer Relief Fund
89 Albert Embankment
London SE1 7UQ
Helpline: 0808 808 2020
www.macmillan.org.uk

Mailing Preference Service (MPS)
DMA House
70 Margaret Street
London W1W 8SS
Tel: 020 7291 3310
www.mpsonline.org.uk

Miscarriage Association
c/o Clayton Hospital
Northgate, Wakefield
West Yorkshire WF1 3JS
Tel: 01924 200799
www.miscarriageassociation.org.uk

National Association for Pre-paid
Funeral Plans (NAPFP)
618 Warwick Road
Solihull
West Midlands B91 1AA
Tel: 0121 711 1343
www.napfp.co.uk

National Association of Funeral
Directors (NAFD)
618 Warwick Road
Solihull
West Midlands B91 1AA
Tel: 0845 230 1343
www.nafd.org.uk

National Association of Memorial
Masons
27a Albert Street
Rugby
Warwickshire CV21 2SG
Tel: 01788 542264
www.namm.org.uk

National Association of Widows
48 Queens Road
Coventry CV1 3EH
Tel: 024 7663 4848
www.nawidows.org.uk

National Council for Voluntary
Organisations
Regent's Wharf
8 All Saints Street
London N1 9RL
Tel: 020 7713 6161
www.ncvo-vol.org.uk

National Funerals College
Professor Malcolm Johnson
Leyton House
6 Warwick Road
Bristol BS6 6HE
Tel: 0117 973 0045

National Secular Society
25 Red Lion Square
London WC1R 4RL
Tel: 020 7404 3126
www.secularism.org.uk

Natural Death Centre
6 Blackstock Mews
Blackstock Road
London N4 2BT
Tel: 087) 288 2098
www.naturaldeath.org.uk

NHS Organ Donor Register
UK Transplant (UKT)
Fox Den Road
Stoke Gifford
Bristol BS34 8RR
Tel: 0117 975 7575

NHS Organ Donor Registration Service
Tel: 0845 606 0400
www.uktransplant.org.uk

Oddfellows Friendly Society
Oddfellows House
40 Fountain Street
Manchester M2 2AB
Tel: 0800 028 1810
www.oddfellows.co.uk

Oyez Straker
Oyez House, 16 Third Avenue
Denbigh West Industrial Estate
Bletchley
Milton Keynes MK1 1TG
Tel: 01908 361166
www.oyezstraker.co.uk

The Pension Service
Tyne View Park
Whitley Road
Newcastle upon Tyne NE98 1YJ
Tel: 0845 606 0265
www.dwp.gov.uk
www.thepensionservice.gov.uk

The Principal Probate Registry
First Avenue House
42–49 High Holborn
London WC1V6NP
Tel: 020 7947 6939
Helpline: 0845 302 0900
Orderline for probate forms and
guidance notes: 020 7947 6983
www.courtservice.gov.uk

Probate and Matrimonial Office
Royal Courts of Justice
PO Box 410
Chichester Street
Belfast BT1 3JF
Tel: 028 9023 5 111
www.courtsni.gov.uk

Public Search Room
Family Records Centre
1 Myddleton Street
London EC1R 1UW
Tel: 0845 603 7788
www.gro.gov.uk

Rationalist Press Association
1 Gower Street
London WC1E 6HD
Tel: 020 7436 1151
www.newhumanist.org.uk

Registers of Scotland
Customer Service Centre
9 George Square
Glasgow G2 1DY
Tel: 0845 6070163
www.ros.gov.uk

Registrar General (Northern Ireland)
Oxford House
49–55 Chichester Street
Belfast BT1 4HL
Tel: 028 9025 2163
028 9025 2000 (credit card line)
www.groni.gov.uk

Registry of Shipping and Seamen
MCA Cardiff
Anchor Court
Ocean Way
Cardiff CF24 5JW
Tel: 029 2044 8800
www.mcga.gov.uk/c4mca/mcga-
seafarer_information/mcga-rss-home.htm

Royal National Institute for the Blind
(RNIB)
105 Judd Street
London WC1H 9NE
Tel: 020 7388 1266
Helpline: 0845 766 9999
www.rnib.org.u

Samaritans
Helpline: 0845 790 9090
www.samaritans.org
Look in your telephone book for local
branch

Scottish Executive Health
St Andrews House
Regent Road
Edinburgh EH1 3DG
Tel: 0131 556 8400
www.scotland.gov.uk

Sea Fisheries Inspectorate
Room 13, East Block
10 Whitehall Place
London SW1A 2HH
Tel: 020 7270 8328
Helpdesk: 0845 933 5577
www.defra.gov.uk

Sheriff Clerks' Office
Commissary Department
27 Chambers Street
Edinburgh EH1 1LB
Tel: 0131 225 2525

Society of Allied and Independent
Funeral Directors (SAIF)
3 Bullfields
Sawbridgeworth
Hertfordshire CM21 9DB
Tel: 0845 230 6777
www.saif.org.uk

South Place Ethical Society
Conway Hall
25 Red Lion Square
London WC1R 4RL
Tel: 020 7242 8037/4
www.ethicalsoc.org.uk

Stillbirth and Neonatal Death Society
(SANDS)
28 Portland Place
London W1B 1LY
Tel: 020 7436 7940
Helpline: 020 7436 5881
www.uk-sands.org

Support after Murder and
Manslaughter (SAMM)
Cranmer House
39 Brixton Road
London SW9 6DZ
Tel: 020 7735 3838
www.samm.org.uk

Index

219

Help at hand – Which? Legal Service

If you have ever been faced with the sort of problems described in this book, you'll be glad to know that Which? has a service, open to all, which allows you to consult some of the UK's top consumer lawyers by telephone at any time Monday–Friday (9am–5pm).

Which? Legal Service offers immediate access to first class legal advice at unrivalled value. Members of this service get practical and sound legal advice, delivered in a user friendly way. The advice covers problems with goods and services, employment law, holiday issues, parking/speeding/clamping offences, probate administration and small business contracts. Each membership gives an entire household the right to call as often as they like during the year – all for a very modest membership cost.

For details of how to join Which? Legal Service, either write to Which?, Gascoyne Way, Hertford X, SG14 1LH, telephone free on (0800) 252100 or visit www.which.co.uk.

Which? is the leading independent consumer champion in the UK.
A not-for-profit organisation, we exist to make individuals as powerful as the
organisations they deal with in everyday life. The next few pages give you a
taster of our many products and services. For more information, log onto
www.which.co.uk or call 0800 252 100.

Which? magazine

Which? is, quite simply, the most trusted magazine in the UK. It takes the stress
out of your buying decisions by offering independent, thoroughly researched advice
on consumer goods and services from cars to current accounts via coffee makers.
Its Best Buy recommendations are the gold standards in making sound and safe
purchases across the nation. Which? has been making things happen for all
consumers since 1957 – and you can join us by subscribing at www.which.co.uk
or calling 0800 252 100 and quoting 'Which'.

Which? online

www.which.co.uk gives you access to all Which? content online. Updated daily, you
can read hundreds of product reports and Best Buy recommendations, keep up to date
with Which? campaigns, compare products, use our financial planning tools and
interactive car-buying guide. You can also access all the reviews from the *The Which?
Good Food Guide*, ask an expert in our interactive forums, register for e-mail updates
and browse our online shop – so what are you waiting for? www.which.co.uk.

Gardening Which?

If you're passionate about gardening, then you'll love *Gardening Which?* Every month,
this informative and inspirational magazine brings you 70 pages of the best plants,
products and techniques, all backed by expert research and stunning photography.
Whatever type of gardener you are, we've got all the advice to make your life easier –
and because it's published by Which? you know it's advice you can trust. To find out
more about *Gardening Which?* log on to www.which.co.uk or call 0800 252 100 and
quote 'Gardening'.

Which? Books

Other books in this series

Which? Essential Guides
The Pension Handbook
Jonquil Lowe
ISBN: 978-1844-900-251/1-84490-025-8

A definitive guide to sorting out your pension, whether you're deliberating over SERPs/S2Ps, organising a personal pension or moving schemes. Cutting through confusion and dispelling apathy, Jonquil Lowe provides up-to-date advice on how to maximise your savings and provide for the future.

Which? Essential Guides
Buying Property Abroad
Jeremy Davies
ISBN: 978-1844-900-244/1-84490-024-X

A complete guide to the legal, financial and practical aspects of buying property abroad. This book provides down-to-earth advice on how the buying process differs from the UK, and how to negotiate contracts, commission surveys, and employ lawyers and architects. Practical tips on currency deals and taxes – and how to command the best rent – all ensure you can buy abroad with total peace of mind.

Which? Essential Guides
Buy, Sell & Move House
Kate Faulkner
ISBN: 978-1-84450-030-5/1-84490-030-4

A complete, no-nonsense guide to negotiating the property maze and making your move as painless as possible. From dealing with estate agents to chasing solicitors, working out the true cost of your move to understanding Home Information Packs, this guide tells you how to keep things on track and avoid painful sticking points.

Which? Essential Guides
Renting and Letting
Kate Faulkner
ISBN: 978-1844-900-299/1-84490-029-0

A practical guide for landlords, tenants, and anybody considering the buy-to-let market. Covering all the legal and financial matters, including tax, record-keeping and mortgages, as well as disputes, deposits and security, this book provides comprehensive advice for anybody involved in renting property.

Which? Books

Which? Books provide impartial, expert advice on everyday matters from finance to law, property to major life events. We also publish the country's most trusted restaurant guide, *The Which? Good Food Guide*. To find out more about Which? Books, log on to www.which.co.uk or call 01903 828557.

❝Which? tackles the issues that really matter to consumers and gives you the advice and active support you need to buy the right products.**❞**